The E-Code

The E-Code

33 INTERNET SUPERSTARS
REVEAL 43 WAYS
TO MAKE MONEY ONLINE
ALMOST INSTANTLY—
USING ONLY E-MAIL!

Joe Vitale and Jo Han Mok

WILEY

John Wiley & Sons, Inc.

Published by John Wiley & Sons, Inc., Hoboken, New Jersey.
Published simultaneously in Canada.

For general information on our other products and services please contact our Customer Care Department within the United States at (800) 762-2974, outside the United States at (317) 572-3993 or fax (317) 572-4002.

Wiley also publishes its books in a variety of electronic formats. Some content that appears in print may not be available in electronic books. For more information about Wiley products, visit our web site at www.Wiley.com.

Library of Congress Cataloging-in-Publication Data:
Vitale, Joe, 1953–
    The e-code : 34 internet superstars reveal 44 ways to make money online almost instantly—using only e-mail! / Joe Vitale, Jo Han Mok.
        p. cm.
    ISBN 0-471-71855-6 (pbk.)
    1. Internet marketing. 2. Internet advertising. I. Mok, Jo Han. II. Title.
    HF5415.1265.V583 2005
    658.8'72—dc22

                                                            2004025809

Printed in the United States of America.

10 9 8 7 6 5 4

Dedicated to my love, Nerissa.
—Joe Vitale

Dedicated to all future E-code practitioners,
my family, and loved ones.
—Jo Han Mok

Contents

Preface

What Is the E-Code?

The E-code unlocks the vault to e-riches. Gaining access to the E-code is the one way left for the little guy to get rich! Decoded, the E-code reads like this in plain English: The right e-message to the right e-crowd at the right time through e-mail! It's not a new principle. It's a logical e-application of the principle governing successful offline direct response marketing.

How did I discover this code? I stumbled on it when I signed up for Joe Vitale's "News You Can Use" at www.MrFire.com. You can see it in action too, simply by signing up for his newsletter yourself. All I did was to make a careful, studied observation of how Joe did his marketing. There it was, the E-code in practice. If you're on his list, you'll find it practically *impossible* to resist buying anything Joe recommends.

Why? It's the E-code at work. It's *that* powerful.

However, Joe is not the only one putting the E-code into practice. Others are doing it too, and getting ridiculous results! Skeptical? Try this: Sign up for Armand Morin's "Big Newsletter" at www.Go Generator.com. I dare you not to buy everything he puts out! You can try, but you won't be able to resist. Why? It's the E-code at work.

The dot bombs happened because they lost all their money on hitting useless targets with meaningless messages. The little guy, with his limited finances and resources, is forced to be wiser—to practice smart resource allocation and discriminate in his marketing. This means excluding the masses and delivering the marketing message to a carefully selected minority of high-probability prospects. Therefore, the most precious commodity online is not your web site, or anything else for that matter. It's your customer's e-mail address!

Regardless of what product or service is being sold, every business should be supersensitive to capturing names. If you've read Russell Conwell's *Acres of Diamonds,* you'll realize that most people look everywhere for opportunity, happiness, and so on, except under their own feet, where they are most likely to find it. Jay Abraham (who probably needs no introduction) makes a fortune by going into established businesses and helping them locate their hidden gold mine: their own customers, who are undervalued and grossly overneglected. Your customer's e-mail address is a jewel that you should polish till it sparkles!

But what if you do not have an existing customer database of e-mail addresses to work with? It's simple. You farm them.

Farming is a marketing term derived from the real estate profession. What it means is simply taking a small, carefully selected target market and nurturing it with frequent, repetitive contacts and exposure, so as to become the dominant presence in your category of business, in as short a time as possible.

Think "big fish, small pond." Not doing so is as good as spitting in the Pacific Ocean. Your target market should be small enough for you to comfortably make an impact on it with the resources you can and will commit.

Ideally, you'll want to find a group of people who have lots of disposable income and are frustrated! They should have problems so big and intense that they toss and turn around at night, sleepless and frustrated as hell.

That's right, the key word is *frustration.* You can get anything in life by helping people get what they want. Our income level is commensurate with the difficulty level of problems that we solve. When we solve small problems, we get paid small money. Conversely, when we solve big problems, we get big money.

That's the beauty of the E-code. It works on this premise: Identify the market, build and develop an offer around solving the problems that market faces, and deliver the message. It's much better than shooting blanks aimlessly.

Here are the 10 best ways to apply the E-code:

1. Increase the number of offers made to the target market.
2. Offer new products and services.
3. Encourage increased consumption of your product/service.
4. Establish your role as a value provider by giving useable free information.
5. Conduct surveys to identify other problems so that you'll get new ideas for products.
6. Segregate your existing database by separating customers from prospects and suspects.
7. Identify hyperresponsive customers.
8. Encourage and reward hyperresponsiveness.
9. Sell a continuity type of program, such as membership.
10. Upgrade suspects to prospects, prospects to customers, and existing customers to hyperresponsive ones.

This is just a macro view of the E-code, but I believe it may have set your mental cash register ringing away like crazy.

Thrilled? I'm sure you are. It gets even better! The best practitioners of the E-code, the ones who walk the talk, are all assembled within the folds of this book to give you the right combination to dial to access it. Cover to cover, this could be the most valuable moneymaking information you'll ever feast your eyes on. You're in for a real treat. Let's go!

Jo Han Mok, in partnership with Dr. Joe Vitale
Midas Touch Marketing
http://www.PowerAffiliateMarketing.com

Introduction

Follow the steps, ideas, insights, tips, tricks, and stories in this book and you can be making good money online within only 30 days—or even less. The book you are holding is an example of how anyone can make money fast using the Internet and a simple e-mail account. That's right. You don't even need a web site to make e-money.

Let me explain. I met Jo Han Mok in Dallas the weekend of February 1, 2003. Jo Han was then a 23-year-old music student from Singapore living in Boston. I've rarely seen any youth with the kind of energy, drive, commitment, friendliness, snap, and integrity that I see in Jo Han. He's a whirlwind. He's a genius. And he's a nice guy, too.

He e-mailed me after the Dallas event and suggested we work on a book together. I have written several books and didn't need another one. But I liked Jo Han, and I agreed. I suggested that we make our book on the topic of how to make money almost instantly online, using simple e-mail, and that we write it for newbies.

Jo Han loved the idea. He also said we could do the book by not writing all of it. I liked that idea. He said he would write to online experts and ask them to contribute their suggestions, tips, and so forth. It would be a kind of *Chicken Soup for the Soul* approach: Let others write the book. I said I would do the same.

Within a few hours we had sent out e-mails to all the leading Internet marketers and business people we could think of. A few hours later we started to receive their contributions. And only a few days later—less than one week—we had most of this book done. Since you are now reading the finished book, you can see that our simple plan worked.

Now stop and think about this:

➤ Jo Han and I came up with the idea and shared our refinements—by e-mail.

➤ We wrote to people and asked for their contributions—by e-mail.

➤ We received, shared, polished, and rewrote the material—all by e-mail.

➤ I wrote and will send this introduction to Jo Han—again by e-mail.

➤ And after that, we'll send all of our files to the printer—again, by e-mail.

In short, we created this book in less than one month and by using only e-mail and other people's ideas. We barely did any work. The only real cost of the original, self-published book was printing, and we could have skipped that fee by releasing it as an e-book. But because we want to make this book a number one best-seller on Amazon.com (which we'll do with an e-mail-only marketing campaign), we chose to print it.

You can do this, too. And you can do better than this.

For example, some months ago I met Andrei Aleinikov, author of the great book *MegaCreativity*. He told me how he won the Guinness World Record for creating and publishing a book in the shortest time in history. The book is titled *Making the Impossible Possible*. It was written and published in only 15 hours and 46 minutes.

How did he do it? He was at a seminar in Africa on October 10, 2001, with 200 other attendees. Each was asked to come up with an idea, in less than five minutes, on how to make the impossible possible. All of the ideas were gathered, e-mailed to a printer, and published the very same day. Every attendee and contributor went home with a copy of the book. You can imagine how good *that* felt.

I'm telling you, miracles are possible. All you have to do is expand your mind. All you have to do is believe anything is possible. All you have to do is read this book and reflect on the ideas in it. And all you need is Internet access and a simple e-mail account.

You can come up with a better idea than Jo Han or I, or any of the contributors to this book. And even if you don't right away, you can use any of the ideas in this book to make easy e-money fast.

Who will be the next superstar online? Who will break the records for making e-money fast? Who will retire rich next because of passive e-income? I'm betting it will be you.

Go for it!

Joe Vitale
President, Hypnotic Marketing, Inc.
http://www.mrfire.com

The E-Code

1

How to Make Money *Fast* Online

Joe Vitale

Don't throw in the towel. I know you've been reading about people making money online. I know you've tried to do it. Well, don't give up just yet. I have a plan to help you make at least some money on the Internet, and I'm going to give it to you right now.

Here's my online money formula in brief: Basically, find out what this week's most popular searches are at Google. Then pick one of them and quickly generate an e-book, e-report, or even e-audio related to that subject. Put up a site and start selling. List one copy on eBay. That's it.

Here's how it works in five simple steps:

1. Go to http://www.google.com/press/zeitgeist.html and see what the hot searches are currently.

2. Pick one of them that you are at least somewhat curious about.

3. Research the subject online, compiling information about it. This will be your e-product. Be creative. Develop something people searching on this topic will want. (Get help on how to create e-books fast at www.7dayebook.com.)

4. Then quickly put up a one-page web site and offer your e-product for sale. You can put up sites at http://www.GoDaddy.com (a one-page site there is only $14.95 a year).

5. List one copy of your product on eBay. This will get your product and site noticed right away by millions of people.

In short, you're riding the wave of the public's interest.

This is a tried-and-true moneymaking secret. For example, on Easter a friend showed me a book of nothing but questions and answers about the movie *The Passion of the Christ*. The book is compiled data. Yet because it ties to the current frenzy of interest in Mel Gibson's movie, the book is selling and the author is getting on national TV and radio shows.

Cindy Cashman recently used this same idea to create two e-books that are a spin-off of Donald Trump's current TV show *The Apprentice*. See www.CindyCashman.com. Unless Trump actually trademarks the phrases "You're hired!" and "You're fired!" Cindy is going to profit from Trump's stardom.

You can do this, too. Simply create something that ties to an existing popular search and use the above steps to jump-start your sales.

For example, one week in April 2004, one of the top searches was for "IRS." Obviously, if you had information to help people deal with the IRS, you could capitalize on it. But if you didn't have any info, you could search the Internet for it, find an angle that is fresh, and release your own IRS product.

Another week the name "Elisha Cuthbert" was a top-10 search item. You could compile a directory of all the sites showing pictures of the actress; compile quotes by her; or maybe create an Elisha Cuthbert cookbook, beauty tips guide, joke book, or whatever, based on your Web searches. Or you could go contrarian and create something called "Why I Hate Elisha Cuthbert." (I don't. I think she's a great actress in the TV show *24* and I hear she's a nice person, too.) You could also get outrageous and create a campaign called "Elisha Cuthbert for President." Your site could sell an e-book where you offer Elisha as a candidate.

Get the idea? Not everyone reading this article will act on this formula, but those who do have a good chance of making a lot of money fast. Will you be one of them?

2

Top 10 Laws of Internet Marketing

Randy Charach

■ THE FOUNDATION

The number one determination as to whether you will be successful as an Internet marketer is how you relate to people. Read that again, especially if you are shocked to hear this. It is the key to your success in all that you do.

What—likeable? I thought I would be anonymous, hiding behind my computer, without ever having to directly relate to any of my customers. Dream on, friend. That is not reality. And even though it is possible to avoid contact, your true nature will come out in your writing and/or marketing and greatly affect your profits.

Now, ask yourself: Are you likeable? Do you have genuine concern for the welfare of your customers and suppliers? Do your actions demonstrate your concern for providing excellent service and value? Do you pleasantly surprise people by delivering more than what is promised? Do you show appreciation to those who support you?

Or are you grumpy and money hungry? Do you use whatever tactics are available to make a sale? Do you take the money and run?

Be honest, and don't feel badly if you don't like your answers. You can change and improve your practices over time. There are people who make money without being kind and conscientious, but they do it the hard and unpleasant way. All else being equal, they will make less money for shorter duration and ultimately will be unfulfilled on many levels.

If relating to people does not come naturally to you, then try harder. Adopt a more caring attitude bit by bit, day by day, and you will be rewarded both financially and spiritually. The transformation will come naturally as you apply gentle and mindful attention to your actions.

■ RESPECT + CREDIBILITY = HAPPIER CUSTOMERS AND HIGHER PROFITS

Imagine you are surfing the Web for information and sifting through many sites that seem quite interesting to you. There are many similarities among e-books for sale, and although you were looking for free information, you decide to spend a few bucks to get information that is fresh, innovated, and not free. Consider the following scenario.

Digital Product A
➤ The site loads slowly.
➤ There are pop-up windows for everything from Viagra to on-line casinos.
➤ Looks like good information but you are skeptical of some of the claims.
➤ Cost is $19.

Digital Product B
➤ The site loads quickly.
➤ There is one pop-up offer from the author of the site offering a free e-zine.
➤ Looks like good information and the claims are credible.
➤ Cost is $149.

Digital Product C

➤ Same as product B, but also includes extras that would cost several hundred dollars to purchase separately. You can use the extras immediately, and they perfectly complement the main product.

➤ Cost is $199.

All other factors (and there are many that we will soon cover) being equal, which are you going to buy? Well, there is a market for all the choices above. And when presented with most of the important elements in place, they all can do well.

Yes, even product A can make money. Not that you would want it, since there are much better alternatives. Many people promote things like product A and miss out on a great opportunity. They don't understand the importance and methods of adding value and respecting their web site visitors. It's a numbers game, and there are people who want or need to pay less and either can overlook or will not notice various downfalls.

Let me ask you a question that was often posed by my dear father when I was younger. My dad, by the way, is in his 80s and, although retired now for 20 years, is a master salesman (and always has a joke to share).

My father asked me this: Would you rather pay a little more and get a lot more? or pay a little less and get a lot less? If the product you are considering buying is designed to make you more money, and you will make a lot more money because of the built-in extras and the added bonuses, you will be willing to pay a bit more. Right?

I will show you how to add great value to your product with little extra effort and no cost to you.

Remember the equation that opened this section: Respect + credibility = Happier customers and higher profits. Well, how does that translate?

In the previous examples, there is a lack of respect by the site owner in product A. The site loads slowly and disrespects the time of the visitor. Further disrespect is added by the volume and nature of the pop-ups. If a site fails to establish credibility, then it will most likely fail to attract customers and higher profits. This truism is more important as each day passes and people become more and more weary of scammers.

Product B earns respect, or at least doesn't instantly lose it, and it is favored by prospects because of its quick load speed. It establishes credibility by displaying testimonials and backing up major claims. Product C is creating greater profit for the seller while providing greater value and appeal to most potential buyers.

I asked you earlier which product you would buy. Now, let me ask you another question. Which seller are you or would you like to be?

What we are examining here may sound simple, and indeed the examples are. But the principle, the underlying message, is so important for you to embrace that failing to do so will make a huge impact on your bottom line and well-being. Do not skip or rush through this section and the following principles. You will be doing yourself a great disservice, regardless of your current level of marketing and business skill.

Do you get the point? You will sell more products and services at higher prices and get greater satisfaction by being great to deal with. And you will further increase your profits by being resourceful and adding value to your customers.

There are certain specific traits that successful people share. Some will come naturally to you, others you will learn. Some you will not agree with, or like, and will resist. These are the ones you need to work on the most. You see, the traits you are uncomfortable with are the ones that have been holding you back. They will be the hardest to understand or accept, for a combination of reasons. Be willing to step outside your comfort zone if necessary.

The following is a description of some of the traits I want you to think about and start working on now.

■ TOP 10 SUCCESSFUL INTERNET MARKETING LAWS

By following these 10 principles, you will develop the key traits that lead quickly to success.

➤ Always Tell the Truth

You don't need a great memory if you are always honest. You lose all credibility when you are caught in a lie. Telling lies on the Internet by making up testimonials or otherwise enhancing your claims will very quickly end your career.

When you go to a web site and see testimonials like this:

"Your product was worth 10 times what I paid."—TC, Blaine, WA

What comes to mind? "Who the hell is TC?" Right? Is the marketer just making up testimonials? Perhaps TC is hiding under the federal witness protection program. Yes, that's it! That is why we can't know the person's full name.

Or how about this one:

"Your product was worth 10 times what I paid."—John Smith

Hmmm, wonder where John is from? Another mystery to solve!

Look, we see this type of thing all the time. These examples are not even far-fetched or hypothetical. Examine everything you do and all the claims you make with a skeptical mind. Make sure you can back up your claims, and always present yourself and your offers in a manner that is believable. When appropriate, provide proof.

➤ Be a Fair Negotiator

On a close-in, personal level, you negotiate with your friends when discussing what movie to see or which restaurant to eat at. On the other end of the scale, you will negotiate joint venture arrangements with other marketers.

There are many areas in which you can negotiate lower pricing and better terms for the goods and services that you will require as you market products on the Internet. In addition, successful Internet marketers learn to trade and to barter their goods and services with others who are doing business on the Web. Not only does this help you maximize your profits, it will also open the door to many new opportunities that you would otherwise miss.

The Internet is an interesting place to do business. Many of the products offered for sale are digital. Many of the services require an initial start-up cost on the part of the business owner. Once the initial and monthly expenses are covered, most of the money that comes in is profit. This is the perfect environment for people like you and me who are in a similar business situation to open the door to negotiation. We often have no hard cost to absorb when trading our products.

Let me give you an example. A few months ago I received an e-mail from a young man who happens to live in Texas. He is 16 years old and wanted to pick up the master rights to a product that he saw me advertise for sale at one of my web sites. It sells for $249. He directed me to a site where he offers the service of creating e-book covers. I sent him the digital product he wanted, he made a few covers for me, and we both are happy. (Note: He has since pulled the site, as he is too busy with school.)

I could fill a whole book with examples, but you get the point, right? Present and receive requests for barter and concessions in a fair and polite manner. Never grind or be unpleasant to deal with.

In this particular instance, my personal feeling is that persistence is not the key. Many would disagree, and in most cases you ought to be persistent, but not when asking someone else to trade or give you something. Be classy about it and don't take rejection personally. No one will think less of you just for asking, and as a matter of fact, some of my strongest alliances have been formed as a result of an initial trade of goods or services.

➤ Live by the Golden Rule, but Go Beyond to the Platinum Rule

The golden rule, "Do unto others as you would have done unto yourself," may not apply in every case. What pleases me may not please you. You must also understand how the other person wants to be "done unto," and act accordingly.

It's unrealistic to believe that you can simply set up a web site, then go on vacation, return in a month, and discover that you have sold thousands of dollars worth of your product without providing any customer service. Don't get me wrong—it's *close* to being realistic, and that is one of the many reasons I love this business. But no matter how much you automate your daily tasks, there will always be a need for you or someone who works for you to communicate with prospects and customers.

I certainly encourage you to automate tasks and set up systems in order to minimize time spent on activities that can possibly avoid individual personal attention. But when you find yourself dealing with people directly, be sure to listen carefully to what they say. Observe closely the words they use, and respond accordingly.

My experience as a consumer of digital products on the Internet has been quite varied. Those companies that have been thoughtful and responded to simple requests for clarification have earned much of my business.

On the other side of the scale, I know that I have been successful selling more products and services on the Internet because I treat every person in a manner that is thoughtful and considerate of individual needs and desires.

➤ Overpromise and Overdeliver

Offer and deliver so much that your offer is irresistible. If we don't convince others to do business with us, there is no opportunity to overdeliver. Of course, you must deliver even more than promised in every area of your service and product.

There is just way too much competition on the Internet from people like you and me, who are vying for people's hard-earned money in exchange for information. We cannot ignore the concept of overdelivering.

➤ If You Can't Join Them, Beat Them

I am all for cooperating with like-minded people. Joint ventures and cooperative marketing efforts can be terrific. You may find, however, that unless you take control and become a strong leading force, you will have to work under other people's terms.

You really ought to only target markets where people are already successfully selling products to the customers within the market under consideration. Try to make alliances with these people and set up joint ventures and endorsed marketing efforts through affiliate programs and other reciprocal agreements.

Become a strong competitor. Pick the leaders in the specific area you are pursuing and strive to be better. But do so with utmost respect for these other marketers, and allow them to enjoy your profits and success along with you.

➤ If You're Not Early, You're Late

Within a few seconds from now, any number of the many marketers out there can send an e-mail to their customer and prospect lists of hundreds, thousands, or tens of thousands of subscribers. If that e-mail contains information about a hot new opportunity for the readers, not only will the owner of the list grab the lion's share of profits to be made, but he or she will be seen as being on the ball, and the subscribers will place greater value in being on that owner's list.

More than any other business I can think of, Internet marketers must be on top of current trends and make timely offers that will appeal to their specific target market. Better yet, and in addition, why not lead some of those trends and create some of those hot products yourself?

➤ Be Eclectic

There is rarely one right way to do anything. There is no rule saying that you or I have to choose only one way to generate business, or to do anything, for that matter. A variety of approaches will often be most effective. Apply this thinking to everything you do.

Be diversified in your pursuit to deliver information products to niche markets. This is key to your success. It will be your job both to infiltrate a variety of areas and to become knowledgeable in specific areas. As you enter these different groups—and of course, I recommend you start with one that you are already familiar with or at least have a keen interest in—you want to be eclectic once again. In other words, develop the habit of widening your interests and then broadening your knowledge and skills within those interests.

The information you're going to provide by way of your products will only be of value when it is targeted and narrowly focused. It is your job to be resourceful where others are not, in researching specific points of information that will provide specific benefits to specific groups of people. In order to do that, you identify the problems of the group and provide solutions to those problems.

➤ Educate Yourself

Acquiring knowledge can be your single best return on investment (ROI)—assuming you apply the information. You must turn what you learn into a skill or greater understanding by acting upon what you learn. Invest in books, courses, manuals, and trainings that apply to all aspects of marketing, whether directly or indirectly related to the Internet. You will save thousands of dollars and a lot of time by learning from other people's mistakes and successes.

Be sure to digest new information every single day and integrate what you learn into your thinking and your actions. Then, when it comes to writing your own materials, your vocabulary, thoughts, ideas, and experiences will be much fuller.

➤ Listen More and Talk Less

I am constantly amazed at how people love the sound of their own voice. Remember, you already know what you are going to say and can therefore learn little by talking. Allow other people you encounter to share their thoughts and ideas with you. Regardless of who they are or how much or little you think they know, you can learn something from everyone.

Be willing to reciprocate with your information, but you will seldom be asked or given a chance to talk by most people. You have two ears and one mouth. Use them in that proportion and prosper.

When does this apply? Listening carefully applies to written correspondence, too. Answer e-mail questions only after truly understanding what is being asked. I find many people do not practice this at all. Don't you? Frustrating, isn't it?

➤ Be Balanced

This is a tough one for me. I am currently obsessed with doing business on the Internet. It is often a struggle to spend time on anything else. Perhaps you are the same way.

Still, I develop other interests, exercise regularly, study many topics, and try to be a well-rounded individual. I have learned to expand my interests and, as you just read in the section about being eclectic, that balance of interests can really pay off. Do not neglect your health and family for the sake of work. It will cost you dearly in all areas of your life.

There are two other important principles to share with you in this lesson. They go hand in hand and are crucial to your success in this business.

1. Diversify and adapt.
2. Constantly promote your products and services.

Please do not mistake diversification as being the opposite of single-minded focus and specialization. Instead, understand this to mean that you will prosper and grow in many ways by broadening your services as you monitor the needs of your clients. Learn and develop new knowledge and skills as a marketer and merchant of information.

It is essential to your success as an Internet marketer to constantly remind people to use your services. Your products and e-zines are advertisements for your other products and affiliate items. They are vehicles for selling your other products and services. This does not mean that you cheapen your offerings by any means in order to sell more. On the contrary, your excellent products and services are powerful sales mechanisms in creating more business as you provide more value to your customers.

Satisfy your customers' needs and provide excellent value, service, and information that they cannot get elsewhere. Then do them a service and feed them more of this good stuff.

Randy Charach is one of the Internet marketing world's brightest stars. He is a popular seminar speaker and producer of quality information products, and he is a professional magician (www.RandyPromo.com).

In addition to his straight-to-the-point practical advice on making money online, he is known for providing sound philosophical advice that ultimately lays the foundation for greater financial rewards. That is why we have chosen to kick off this book with an excerpt (thanks, Randy) from Randy's best-selling e-book, Niche Magic: How to Pick a Niche and Get Rich *(www.NicheMagic.com).*

To receive Randy Charach's free e-zine on marketing and business opportunities, be sure to visit www.RandyReport.com.

3

Five Explosive Marketing Strategies for Exponential Business Growth

Jo Han Mok

Do you know the answer to this question: "What can you do now to *instantly* increase the profitability of your business?"

Well, the answer is surprising simple: Change your strategy.

Your strategy is the master purpose of your business. It's the fabric that binds your business systems together and the bedrock of your business's entire operating approach.

Here are five instantly deployable strategies that can take your business to new heights, regardless of what product or service you're selling.

■ EXPLOSIVE STRATEGY 1: BIG-PICTURE AWARENESS

Napoleon Hill listed "accurate thought" as one of the most important success principles. Most business owners don't even think about their businesses. They simply adopt a reactive approach.

The truth is, you can't go anywhere unless you know where you're going. And frankly, this is why so many businesses out there fail, because they know not what they're doing.

Try this simple exercise to cultivate big-picture awareness: Get a whole bunch of colored pencils and a sketchpad, and start creating a mind map of your business or next project. You should be able to look at the mind map and instantly know the following:

➤ Who's doing what (for instance, web site design will be done by the webmaster).

➤ The possible options your prospect will take, and the outcomes.

➤ Points of up-sell, down-sell, cross-sell.

In short, you should have every single piece of the puzzle there. Objectively, your strategy should bring you the most results in the shortest period of time on the most sustainable basis. Once your master strategy is in place, everything else is merely tactical.

■ EXPLOSIVE STRATEGY 2: FUNNEL VISION

Always remember: A buyer is a buyer is a buyer. Every business should capitalize on the lifetime value of the customer through expansive repurchases of products and services.

Have a marketing funnel in place. Introduce ancillary products that you deem to be performance enhancing. These can be other people's products that you can obtain from joint venturing. Most importantly, you'll want to graduate your customer to higher-ticket items as high-octane fuel for business growth.

■ EXPLOSIVE STRATEGY 3: THE INNER CIRCLE

You'll find that many people are belongers. Such people tend to pride themselves on being a part of an elite group. They highly value membership and association. The savvy entrepreneur will do well to take advantage of such behavioral traits and cater to this select group.

There is a threefold advantage in doing so. First, it's a highly efficient way to bundle goods or services together. Second, it's a great way to introduce continuity in your business. And last but not least, it encourages hyperresponsiveness.

■ EXPLOSIVE STRATEGY 4:
IDENTIFYING HYPERRESPONSIVENESS

Have you ever encountered customers who seem to buy almost anything you put out? Customers who seem to be on standby, waiting to grab just about anything new that you put out or recommend? It's a great idea to group such people into an A-list, the high rollers, if you will.

Usually, such people will come from your own database, and it should be your business priority to encourage hyperresponsive behavior. Make sure hyperresponsiveness is always well rewarded with surprise bonuses, freebies, and nurturing communication.

Remember, because of the Pareto principle, 80 percent of your profits will come from 20 percent of your customers. Guess who belongs to the 20 percent?

■ EXPLOSIVE STRATEGY 5:
MULTIPLE INCOME SOURCES

You're practically leaving money on the table if your business is limited to a few channels. Affiliate programs have made it possible for almost any business to make money from ancillary products at a few mouse clicks. Why go through the hassle of product development and the costs associated with it? Remember, you're never in the business of anything, but you're always in the business of marketing the business. And all you have to do as an affiliate, basically, is market.

Though many affiliate programs are free to join, it would always be a good idea to purchase the product in question and do a thorough review first before recommending it. As an information facilitator, you should feel good about recommending a product that you sincerely know will benefit your list, and not be afraid of getting flamed for trying to pitch. If someone is offended and unsubscribes, then just shrug and say "Next." You don't need such people on your list.

There you have it, my "Big Five" strategies for optimal business growth and profitability. Use them, and watch your business take on a new dynamism! A positive side effect may include swelling of your bank account. Best of all, they don't cost a cent to implement, so don't wait. The time is now.

4

Spirit Money: Five Steps to Attract Money When You Have None

Joe Vitale

Dear Joe,

I read your *Spiritual Marketing* book and love it. It's very inspiring. I'm using your five steps to create wealth from the inside out, but I need money *now*. What can you suggest? Thank you.

—Stacey

Stacey's letter resembles the dozens of letters I get every week. They touch my heart. Because I sincerely want to help, I've created the following steps to help you attract money from spirit—right now.

1. *Get the lesson.* As I explained in *Spiritual Marketing* (now titled *The Attractor Factor*), as soon as you get the lesson from your circumstance, the situation will resolve. It will simply correct itself. In other words, if you are broke right now, ask yourself what the lesson in being broke is for you. Don't settle on flip answers, like "I should save more in advance." And don't blame others. It's no one's fault. What is the positive reason for you to have this situation in your life? You know the answer. Be honest and write it down.

2. *Obey the impulse.* You are being nudged from within to do something. I have no idea what that is for you. But you do. It probably scares you. Maybe you're supposed to open a business. Or change jobs. Or start making calls. Or meditate more. Whatever that nudge is, obey it. Act on it. That's what I call "inspired action." You listen to your feelings, that stirring in your heart, and you act on what you hear.

3. *Demand resolution.* You have more power than you imagine. When Jesus healed the sick, he didn't say, "I hope you get better." Instead he said, "Rise and walk." He acted with authority. He declared his demands. In other words, what is your intention for this situation? State it not as a request but as a command. Exert your power. Speak it to the heavens. "I intend to have five hundred dollars by midnight tomorrow night" is more powerful than "I hope I get some money soon."

4. *Give thanks.* Whatever is going on in your life holds a great gift for you. Maybe you can see it, maybe not. But assume it is there and you'll suddenly feel better. You'll breathe a sigh of relief. As soon as you relax, many things will open in you. Your mind may see new opportunities that your tension was blocking. Your body may simply relax, allowing you to get a good night's rest, which we all need to live and work today.

5. *Expect miracles.* I'm constantly amazed at the number of people who say they pray, go to church, or meditate, or in some other way show they believe in divine intervention, yet these same people worry, complain, and act out of fear, not faith. Well, if you truly believed in miracles, wouldn't you relax and look for them? Wouldn't you even expect them? I carry a coin with a mustard seed embedded in it. It reminds me to have faith "like a mustard seed." When you think about it, a mustard seed has no doubt. None. It is clear about what it is. Start being a mustard seed.

5

Missing Links

Gary Vurnum

Nothing can stop the man with the right mental attitude from achieving his goal; nothing on earth can help the man with the wrong mental attitude.

—Thomas Jefferson

You've read the e-books. You've decided on your tactics. You've got your web page. You've got your e-zine. . . . But you aren't making any money! Worse still—you don't know why!

I can tell you why. You might think you have everything in place, but you haven't. You are missing one vital element. The sole difference between success and failure is you! Yes, *you*! You are your own worst enemy. But you don't realize it, and you keep blaming somebody or something else.

Almost everyone I have ever met begins a project before deciding whether if it's really right for them. They *think* that it is, but after a few setbacks they decide that maybe it wasn't appropriate for them after all. The key to anything new you take on in life, whether online or off-line, whether work-related or family driven, is to focus on *you* before the actual project.

You may think that I am talking rubbish, but let me ask you this question: How many negative, miserable, and depressed self-made millionaires have you ever seen? Ask any successful person in any field, and they will tell you that their positive attitude to setbacks was one of their best abilities. How could they react so positively? Their reactions were the result of four things:

1. Their attitude
2. Their belief
3. Their focus
4. Their knowledge

Notice that knowledge comes at the bottom of the list, and not at the top. Here's why: Almost all of the richest and most successful people in the world have had a right-hand man (or woman). Bill Gates had Paul Allen. Steve Jobs had Steve Wozniak. Warren Buffett had Charlie Munger. Sherlock Holmes had Dr. Watson! And I could go on.

"Hold on a minute," you might say. "What about all of those others who did it on their own—such as Richard Branson, Donald Trump, George Soros, Larry Ellison, and all the rest!"

You might think that they did it all on their own, but they all had either an excellent, unsung hero working with them (in Richard Branson's case), or a team of excellent and trusted advisers working on their behalf. So every successful person had someone else who was more knowledgeable than them in the areas where they were weak. In essence, they employed people who are better than them.

"But what's that got to do with a one-man band like me?" you may question. It has *everything* to do with you! Your success in any area is a matter of relationships—the relationship between you and

➤ Your peers.
➤ Your customers.
➤ Your family commitments.
➤ The work you want to do.
➤ That little voice inside your head.

If you don't have access to a mentor or friends who excel at something that you can't do, then you are going to have to teach yourself what you need to achieve success. And I am not talking (initially, anyway) about teaching yourself *how* to do something. I'm talking about teaching yourself *why* to do something. You have to learn the reasons why you want to do something—in other words, what motivates you. This is the principal missing ingredient for your online success!

> *The manager asks how and when; the leader asks what and why.*
>
> —Warren Bennis

In the next few pages I explain in more detail the elements of what could be the difference between your success or failure on the Internet. Let's begin with the first of four missing links.

■ MISSING LINK 1: ATTITUDE

I lose track of the number of people who ask me for coaching advice and use words and phrases like these when they explain why they aren't successful:

➤ "If only . . ."
➤ "I can't . . ."
➤ "It's not my fault . . ."
➤ "I don't have the money . . ."
➤ "I wish . . ."

In all these cases, do you notice that every single one of them passes the buck, either to a lack of something or because of something. These people are never going to be successful, because they have an attitude of lack or failure built into them.

➤ "If only I could write sales pages like Yanik Silver."
➤ "If only I had an e-zine with 150,000 subscribers."
➤ "If only I could make a profit with my advertising."
➤ "If only I could learn HTML."

I, for one:

- ➤ Wrote my web page using Microsoft Word.
- ➤ Had never written a sales letter before I wrote the one for my site (and it shows!).
- ➤ Had never written a line of advertising.
- ➤ Didn't know what an affiliate program was.
- ➤ Had never written anything before (even an article).
- ➤ Had precisely 10 subscribers to my e-zine for the first two weeks.
- ➤ Had never worked for myself.
- ➤ Had never worked from home.

I could go on. What I am trying to say is that despite any lack of skill or talent I may have, it hasn't stopped me from making a reasonable living off of the Internet in a matter of months.

So what's my secret? My secret is . . . I don't have one! All I have is an attitude—a positive one!

"Fat lot of good that will do me," you might say.

Well, all I can say to you is stop reading now. It's not worth your time. Carry on doing what you've always done, and keep getting the same results that you have always got. The simple, most obvious things are always the ones that people ignore because of the very fact that they are simple and obvious.

> *Never ignore the obvious. That's what it is there for.*
>
> —Gary Vurnum

I cannot stress this enough: The single, biggest reason why most people fail in their online businesses is their attitude. You may disagree with me—and of course, you are more than entitled to do that. But show me an individual who has the knowledge, but hasn't got the right attitude, and I'll show you a loser. Show me an individual who has very little knowledge, but a positive, can-do attitude, and I'll show you a winner. Be negative and you will attract negative people and negative things into your life. Be positive and there will be nothing to stop you!

"But . . ." I knew that it was coming! There are no buts.

Let me share with you a quote from the late, great Earl Nightingale. A success guru ahead of his time, he said this sometime in the 1940s and it is as true today as it was then: "You become what you think about."

■ MISSING LINK 2: BELIEF

I *believe* that I will be a millionaire within three years, thanks to the Internet.

There. I've said it. I've announced it to everyone who reads this. I am now accountable to all of you to achieve it. Ah, the pressure! It's fantastic!

> *What we can or cannot do, what we consider possible or impossible, is rarely a function of our true capability. It is more likely a function of our beliefs about who we are.*
>
> —Anthony Robbins

You see, I learned a very valuable lesson a few years ago when I worked for a merchant bank in London. I learned that you are as powerful as you believe yourself to be. That statement may sound a little strange, so let me explain.

I was just a supervisor, working hard for my next promotion. My boss didn't have a clue about what I did, and he liked it that way.

At the end of the year our accounts had to be reconciled with the records of our agents overseas. I disagreed with one of their figures by a cool half million dollars! The trouble was, the figures had been recommended by one of our senior managers—the one who shouted the loudest. So I had a decision to make: Put my signature to figures that I knew were wrong—or let it go. Bear in mind that this decision would affect everybody's year-end bonus (including the senior manager's).

What would you have done? For me, there was no decision to make. I refused to sign off on the figures, and I told the senior manager why.

The chief accountant of the bank went ballistic. Overnight we had lost a half million dollars off of our profit figures. The senior manager made an official complaint to my boss and called in both our internal and external auditors to go through my e-mails and phone calls to establish that I had messed up.

I hadn't. My boss relied on my judgment. Both audits cleared my name. My reputation was left intact after six weeks of intense pressure and scrutiny. The bank made less profit (but at least it was accurate), and the senior manager continued to try to drag my name through the mud for the next year, until I left for another job.

It was after this rather stressful episode in my life that I realized something very valuable for my future online business: If I had the power to go head-to-head with a senior manager and make a decision on a half million dollars, why was I just a supervisor? I also realized that there was no difference between me and someone who was earning a cool $300,000 a year. I now had the *belief* that I could go as far as I wanted to go and be as successful as any of those rich and successful people I looked up to—and I wouldn't be afraid to be involved in such circles.

So when I began my online business, I started e-mailing those people whom others had put on pedestals because of who they were or because of how much they were worth. And you know what? They're just normal people like you and me. And within three years, I will be one of them, too.

You can join me—but only if you really believe that you can, and only if you can *really* see yourself being a guru yourself. But that's the problem for most people—they can't see themselves as one of them, so they never become one. You won't either, unless you can change your opinion of yourself.

I know that it is a very difficult thing to do. I had to go through a very stressful situation to make me realize it! But unless you can really *believe* that you are worth it, you will automatically limit yourself without even realizing it. So make sure that you believe in yourself and your abilities. After all, nobody else can do it for you. It's up to you.

■ MISSING LINK 3: FOCUS

E-mail: It's what made the Internet what it is. It's also the biggest thing working against us as we try to build our business. Why?

Well, what do you do when you first switch on your PC every day? Just a guess—do you check your e-mail? I'll hold my hand up—me too! But, by its very nature, e-mail is a time-eating machine. You read an e-zine in your mail, then click on a link . . . then another from that page, and on and on. Then you have to answer a query from somebody, or reply to someone that you should have replied to the day before.

So what's the answer? Don't do it! Not a great solution—we all know that we have to keep up with e-mail. What I am trying to say, though, is get your priorities right. You might think that checking your e-mail is the most important thing to do as soon as you start working. Wrong! The most important thing to do is *not* to check your e-mail!

Why? Well, let's imagine that in your 9 to 5 job you roll in at 9 every morning, not having the faintest idea about what work you have to do that day. How could you:

➤ Plan?

➤ Measure your output?

➤ Make comparisons with other days?

➤ Know if you were progressing?

➤ Work to your strengths?

➤ Prioritize your work?

I have spent the best part of a couple of hours going through my e-mail, and getting caught up surfing instead of working. It's a killer for a home-based business like mine.

So, at the beginning of every day, sit down and look at what you *need* to do that day. Then begin it!

I couldn't work—why I couldn't even write a single line—when I finally began work at 10:30 every morning. It clicked when I decided one day to leave checking my mail until lunchtime. The results I achieved from those first couple of hours were phenomenal compared to previous days. Why? Because I found it so much easier to remain motivated and *focused* at the very start of my day. Also, I found that I looked forward to surfing, knowing that I had already achieved a lot that day. This one change to my working pattern quadrupled my output overnight. It might not work for you, but it certainly worked for me.

"So . . . what has this really got to do with focus?" you may ask.

Well, I have just used a very common example to highlight how a lack of focused, concentrated effort can have a very serious effect on how much you can achieve. In the Internet age, we are constantly bombarded with technicolor, singing, dancing opportunities that want to take away our time.

This quote from Jim Rohn is one of my all-time favorites: "Time is more valuable than money. You can get more money, but you cannot get more time." When I took it on board and really considered what it meant, it changed the way I think about both my life and my business.

Practically everyone I have ever met (especially on the Internet) is focused on making money. "That's the whole point!" you might say. Err . . . no, it's not. More money is the end result of a concentrated, focused effort of giving some value to someone. That's why all of those get-rich-quick schemes never work. The mistake most people make is that they think they can get something for nothing. Life's not like that.

So you need to focus your efforts on giving something first. The money will follow later. I am not for a moment suggesting that you give away all of your e-books for free, or that you don't charge anything for web design. What I am saying is that nothing in life is free. You have to pay for it somehow, somewhere.

The best way to pay up front is to make sure that *you* are always moving forward and developing. There is no middle ground. You are either moving forward . . . or you are getting left behind. So focus on moving forward every single day. Focus on completing that project. Focus on new ways of presenting your business. Focus on learning something new about your business. Because once you have wasted your time on standing still, you will never be able to get it back.

Stay focused on what you really want from your business and life. Don't get distracted by the next big thing. Focus on what you can do— and do it well. That, my friend, is how most of the gurus got to where they are today. Want to join them?

■ MISSING LINK 4: KNOWLEDGE

This is not really a missing link—it's just a very misused one. For most people, lack of knowledge can be overcome. They buy a book, buy an e-book, read articles, listen to audios. Then they put them away, never to be used again. They rely on their already overcrowded brain to remember everything that they have just read or heard. And that's the biggest problem with knowledge—most people never really remember it.

So let's say you've bought the latest e-book by one of the Internet superstars. You print it out and actually read it all the way through (which is probably more than most people do with e-books!). You finish it. Then you put it in a drawer, or maybe even throw it away.

You have just made the mistake that all people who fail to achieve success make: You don't translate the information into a format that you completely understand.

Every book ever written is just somebody's opinion put on paper—their own personal view of the world, or of Internet marketing, or of multilevel marketing.

They, and they alone, are the only ones who know exactly what they mean by what they write. We all view the world differently from any other person. We do this because of the unique experiences and influences we have had up until this very moment. They all act together as a filter that sits in front of everything we view. These are our conditioning influences.

So in order for us to personalize the knowledge that we are attempting to take on board, we need to translate the information presented to us into our own language. This may sound a little technical, but all I am really trying to say is this: Never, ever just read a book. *Use* it!

Make notes in the margin. Use a highlighter pen to remind you of the parts most important to you. Unfortunately, this already sounds like too much hard work to a lot of people. They're the poor ones.

I am asking that you then do even more work. Go through the book and write out (preferably in some form of permanent notebook or journal) the highlighted passages—and this is the key part—*in your own words!* Whether it is an e-book on Internet marketing, an audiotape on personal development, or a how-to e-zine on writing, translate what you read and hear into your own words! If you do that with every book that you read or tape that you hear, I guarantee that within six months you will have left your peers in the dust.

I know that it can be a difficult thing to do, but take it from me—I believe that this exercise alone has helped me get to where I am today.

> *Just as the largest library, badly arranged, is not so useful as a very moderate one that is well arranged, so the greatest amount of knowledge, if not elaborated by our own thoughts, is worth much less than a far smaller volume that has been abundantly and repeatedly thought over.*
>
> —Arthur Schopenhauer

Don't let a little bit of laziness get in the way of your success. Otherwise you will only have yourself to blame.

Gary Vurnum quit his full-time job to devote himself to his family and self-development. His life turned around after the birth of his severely disabled son. He now shares the tools he learned to survive and remain positive during the worst time of his life. Gary offers mentoring and can be reached at coach@scienceofsuccess.com. You can also visit his web site at www.OurSuccessPartnership.com.

6

Put Back the Power in Your Affiliate Marketing Business!

Ewen Chia

Would you want a simple way to make money like crazy, using other people's time, expertise and effort? If you do, tap onto an online income strategy commonly known as affiliate marketing. It lets you reap constant profits without having your own product, and without even being an expert in the market you're promoting to.

However, as ideal as affiliate marketing is as a money-generating strategy, most affiliates are doing it all wrong. This leads to most of them not making a good enough income to justify their belief and motivation.

As a top affiliate marketer, I made these same mistakes when I first started out. Here are some of the *right* things to do if you want to sell more affiliate products and become a power (or super) affiliate. Apply these five tips to power-charge your affiliate marketing business and put it on the right track to profit. These are especially crucial if you've wandered off track unknowingly.

■ ZOOM RIGHT INTO THE HOT ZONES

You can't sell to everybody. Success comes when you're able to identify and pinpoint the correct market with the purchasing power. Seek a targeted group of people who already want to buy, and align this group to your interest and passion. Spot these hot zones and sell to them. Simply put, the solution is to zoom into mini markets within the general main market. This is an idea similar to niche marketing except what you want are the subniches.

Use a tool like goodkeywords.com to fire in on the hot zones or subniches in the market. Look for people who are already seeking products to solve their problems by using qualifiers like "learn," "buy," and "find." For example, wouldn't a big market like golfers have hot zones like people who are specifically looking for used golf clubs? Do they have the money to buy?

Another excellent resource I can think of is AdWord Analyzer, which really drills into the heart of these hot zones. You can find it at http://www.l1nk.com/urr/awa.html.

■ CREATE MULTIPLE SMALL LISTS TO SERVE YOUR HOT ZONES

All super or power affiliates have their own opt-in lists. Marketing to your own lists is like having the power to print money on demand anytime you want. It's essential to have your own lists.

The trick here again is to build super-segmented lists serving different groups of people who are willing to spend. The more targeted the lists, the more affiliate sales you'll make.

Here's a site of mine using this principle in action: http://www .MarketingEbookReview.com.

■ PROMOTE KEY-FOCUSED PROGRAMS

Just as you can't sell to everyone, you also can't promote every program. Power affiliates know how to seek out the best programs and focus on promoting these key programs.

Create a portfolio of affiliate programs you can depend on. Base your selection process on such criteria as their product quality, conversion rate, commission structure, and reputation. Promote these same products repetitively and you'll get results. Why? Because both you and your prospects will get to know the products better!

One word of advice is to promote only quality products you've reviewed or used yourself, as nothing is worth a quick buck if you lose your credibility.

■ UNDERSTAND SALES PSYCHOLOGY

This is where most affiliates totally miss out. Have you asked yourself why people buy things? This is crucial, even if you're marketing to your own lists. You need to understand the sales psychology behind human behavior. You need to know your hot zones and how to wow your customers.

People buy because they need to solve specific problems, fill their wants, or experience an emotional ride. What problems or needs does your market have that you can fulfill?

Why is this important? If you know which hot buttons to press, you can create killer copy to effortlessly sell tons of products, whether by web page or e-mail.

If you're a bad copywriter and need a system to create winning copy, here's one tool that can make it much quicker and easier for you: http://tinyurl.com/2lp2t.

■ GO FOR RECURRING COMMISSIONS

Effectively leverage your promotions by earning multiple streams of recurring commissions from one-time efforts. This means choosing to get paid every month even if you stop promoting a particular program. These recurring profits can then be reinvested back into your business for further growth.

Your focus should be on residual affiliate products and services such as the following:

Hosting: http://tinyurl.com/24qq7.

Internet marketing solutions: http://tinyurl.com/2hpel.

Lead generation: http://tinyurl.com/ypj6s.

It's easy to earn massive affiliate income if you know what to do. Use these five tips to kick-start your affiliate marketing business on the right path today.

Ewen Chia is the author of the Power Affiliate Marketing™ Manual, *revealing a profit-churning, proven nine-step system to explode your own affiliate sales in record time! Discover how you can become a power affiliate by visiting http://www.PowerAffiliateMarketing.com.*

7

Let Somebody Else Make Your First Product

Charles Burke

One excellent way to create your own product quickly is by doing interviews.

Make a list of some of the experts on the Web (or off-line), people whose specialty falls in your area of interest. Spend a little time researching their sites or writings. Take notes. Then contact them. Go at this gently, and get to know them first before you ask them for an interview. Or look for someone you already know to introduce you. You can also try to find a pet project of theirs; if it interests you, find a way to make a connection. Another approach is to find out where they'll be appearing (seminar or conference), and attend. Make it a point to meet them while you're there.

Regarding the mechanics of interviewing, Radio Shack carries a $5 phone tap gadget that you can use to record phone conversations. It goes into the circuit of the phone handset, and one wire plugs into your tape recorder. Ultra simple. A more advanced unit called Quick-Tap, available for about $60 at www.jkaudio.com, equalizes both sides of the conversation for your recorder.

To transcribe the tape, you can either go to www.elance.com to find transcribers (hint: $2 a page is about right—and always send a *copy* of the tape, not the master), or, if you have more time than money, get a piece of software called Dictation Buddy at www.highcriteria.com. I've used this software to transcribe several of my interviews, and it's very easy to work with.

Doing interviews will give you a series of documents to use as bonuses, as autoresponder reports, or as stand-alone products. You'll be surprised how quickly you can get a project together and going by using this approach.

By the way, here are three secrets of doing good interviews:

1. Pick people who really know what they're talking about.
2. Read and understand what your interviewee has written.
3. Spend some quality time coming up with nontypical questions—the kind that other people never think to ask.

A person who has been interviewed a lot will greatly appreciate being asked interesting questions. And one last tip: To ensure that your interviewees have time to think up good answers, send them the list of questions in advance, with the understanding that the list is intended as just a jumping-off point.

You may be wondering if successful people are really that approachable. The truth is, I've never been refused when asking for an interview—never. Of course, I try to prepare well, but most leaders *want* to help you.

That's it! There's a lot of power in first preparing well, and then just diving in.

Charles Burke once considered himself so unlucky that having four flat tires in one day didn't even seem odd to him. Now his luck has changed. He lives in Japan where he runs three successful web sites dealing with success, luck, and self-motivation. He is the editor of the Sizzling Edge *newsletter (http://www.sizzlingedge.com) and the author of* Acres of Opportunities *(available at http://www.acresofopportunities.com). He also offers a 20-day e-mail course called "Beyond Luck: 20-Day Boot Camp to Success and Good Fortune," at http://www.beyondluck.com.*

8

Five Critical Factors You Must Consider to Make Massive Affiliate Commissions

Alex Tan

How would you like to print money on demand anytime you want?

This is the reality for the thousands who have stumbled upon affiliate marketing. The beauty of affiliate marketing resides in its ability for anyone to make incredible profits without much work, and in as little as two weeks. This means you can literally start from scratch and make quick money online, without first having to create your own products or web site, or write a single ad.

In fact, affiliate marketing is the ideal starting point for new marketers to get their feet wet. It allows them to use other people's time, effort, and resources for their own gain while further educating themselves for future successes. This is why I call affiliate marketing the ultimate "earn as you learn" strategy.

As powerful as affiliate marketing is, there are five critical factors you need to first consider, before jumping into any affiliate program. Not doing so can cost you dearly in lost profits and wasted resources.

1. *Determine your target audience.* To rake in the big affiliate checks, you must first be able to identify and target your audience. This is a simple case of giving people what they want, but many affiliates commit the mistake of offering the wrong product to the wrong crowd. For example, how many sales do you think you'd make if you promoted copywriting products to an audience interested only in networking opportunities? Not many, if any. Pinpoint your audience to maximize your commissions.

2. *Assess the quality of the affiliate product.* A second way that many affiliates blunder is in marketing a product that does not deliver on its promises. It is always advisable to test the product first before recommending it. Not only will this increase your credibility and sales, it helps you promote better because you can provide personal testimonials on the product.

3. *Verify that the sales letter sells.* Study the affiliate owner's web site and sales copy before sending any traffic over. Inquire about its conversion rates and visitor values. A good test is to ask yourself if you would buy the product. It would be a terrible waste of resources to pay for advertising to a merchant's site, only to discover he or she has poor sales copy that does not sell.

4. *Check availability of promotional materials.* Most affiliate programs provide their affiliates with tools to market with. This allows you to save time by simply editing the provided materials to your own voice instead of creating an ad from scratch. You can then focus instead on the marketing. Having more tools equates to more opportunities to get the sales message through effectively. Simply put, the more tools provided, the more chances you will make the sale.

5. *Make sure your promotion will be profitable.* You must consider how much you will be paid in relation to your promotional efforts. A higher commission percentage can be a huge motivation to place higher focus on a particular product in your total portfolio. Alternatively, seek out products with higher-end pricing or those that offer residual income. You would want to profit exponentially from any effort placed.

These pointers are just the tip of the iceberg in the affiliate marketing game. If you desire to become a power affiliate and bank in huge checks consistently from affiliate programs, you must further educate yourself with the knowledge required for perpetual affiliate success!

Alex Tan, of Midas Touch Marketing, is the co-creator of the critically acclaimed Power Affiliate Marketing System, which transforms scraggly rookies into world class affiliate marketers.

Listen to one such rookie's story at http://www.PowerAffiliateMarketing.com.

9

How I Made Over $112,000 Teaching E-Classes

Joe Vitale

One day I pulled up beside a truck delivering new cars. One of the cars on the flatbed made my heart leap and my blood dance. I had never had a piece of machinery turn me on before. This one did. I fell in love.

It was a BMW Z3—a roadster. A hot-rod. One of the sexiest cars ever known to man and made by gods. Okay, maybe I'm overplaying it. But the point is, this car spoke to me. I wanted it, and wanted it bad.

I also knew BMWs are pricey. So the first thing I did was try to win one. I entered two contests where Z3s were the big prizes. I *knew* I would win—I was destined to have that car. But I didn't win. Alas, so much for the laws of chance. It was time to create my future.

So I decided I would just buy the car, and that I would pay cash for it. I had just completed a book on how to create miracles, called *Spiritual Marketing*, and I figured I would prove to myself that I could create a Z3. So I used my own five-step method to get the sexiest car of my hottest dreams.

I began by setting an intention for getting that car. Oprah once said that "Intention rules the earth." I know it's true. My car's license plate holder says, "I am the power of intention." Once you declare that something will be so, you send a signal into the universe that begins to move that something to you, and you to it. Call it real magic. I call it one of the most powerful steps in the spiritual marketing process. From that step alone, miracles can happen.

After I set my intention to have that car, I then acted on the hunches that bubbled up within me and the opportunities that came my way. One day it occurred to me to offer a seminar on the subject of my new book. I could rent a hotel, write a sales letter, and invite everyone I knew on my online and off-line list to it. I could make a killing in a weekend. But then it occurred to me that I don't like to market seminars, that I didn't know if it would sell, that postage and printing to promote it would cost a fortune, and that I'm not such a big fan of speaking in public, anyway.

And here's where the shift occurred: I began to play with the idea that I could hold the seminar online. I would simply announce the "Spiritual Marketing" e-class to my e-mail list. It would cost me zip. If no one signed up, so what? But if they *did* sign up, I could teach the entire class by e-mail. Every week I would send out a lesson and give assignments. The participants would complete them and e-mail them back. I would then comment on their homework. It would all be nice and neat, easy and convenient. Sounded good to me.

I decided to teach five weeks of classes, mainly because there were five chapters in the *Spiritual Marketing* book. I would send out by e-mail one chapter a week as a lesson. I would add assignments to each one to make it a more legitimate course.

Then I wondered, "What should I charge?" I spent a lot of time on this question. Most people give away their e-classes, if they teach them at all. A few charge low fees. But I wanted a BMW Z3. They cost $30,000 to $40,000 each. Yikes!

I decided I wanted 15 people in my class. That was an arbitrary number. I just figured if 15 people actually did their homework over a five-week period, I would have my hands full reviewing it. So, like everything else in the developing of this first e-class, I simply made up the class size. I then divided 15 by how much I wanted to raise for my Z3. If 15 people paid me $2,000 each, I'd have enough to pay for the car in cash. But two grand per person seemed a bit high. So I settled for $1,500 a person.

I then issued a sales pitch/invitation to my e-mail list to sign up for the class. I had at that time about 800 good names on my list—nothing like what I have today. Still, 16 of them immediately signed up for that first e-class. Talk about easy money!

The class was easy to do, too. The students loved the lessons, my assignments, and my feedback. Only one person immediately asked to bow out, saying the class wasn't for him. So I ended up with 15 people after all. I made $22,500 by e-mail. I was happy.

But I didn't stop there. A few weeks later I announced another e-class, this one on how to write, publish, and promote your own e-book. I just followed the same model that already worked: I issued an invitation to my e-mail list, went after 15 people, and charged $1,500 per person for a five-week class. I got 12 paying customers and made $18,000. Boy, was I loving this!

At this point I had been thinking about writing a sequel to my best-selling e-book, *Hypnotic Writing*. But I didn't want to write it and hope it would sell. I wanted to be paid to write it. So I created yet another e-class. This one would be called "Advanced Hypnotic Writing." It would be three weeks long, rather than five, because I wanted to take it easy this time around. (I was getting lazy.) I still charged $1,500 and I still went after 15 people. I then announced the class to my e-mail list.

Here's where something wild happened: Almost 18 people immediately signed up for the class. But when I asked them to pay the $1,500 fee, every single one of them said they thought the class was free! I was stunned. I reread my invitation. It clearly said there was a hefty fee. All I can figure is that people skimmed the letter, got excited, and just shot back e-mails to enroll in the class. Or maybe they read the word "fee" as "free." Go figure.

But that's not the only odd thing that happened with this class: I had trouble filling it from my own e-list. So I went and asked a person with a giant e-mail list if he would promote my class to his people. He said he would—for 50 percent of the pie. Ouch! That was a lot, but I wanted to get paid to write my sequel to *Hypnotic Writing*, and I'd still end up with good money, anyway. So I agreed.

Well, 20 people signed up. And the oddly wonderful thing is that no one—*no* one!—did the assignments. So I got their money (half of it, anyway: $15,000), I got paid to write my *Advanced Hypnotic Writing* e-book, and I had no homework to review or grade. What a cool business!

Then I announced yet another e-class. I was about to buy a large country estate and wanted more money fast. This new class was on my new proprietary marketing formula, called "Guaranteed Outcome Marketing." I raised the price on this five-week e-class to signal its value. I asked for $2,500 per person. Since I normally charged (at that time) $25,000 to create a Guaranteed Outcome Marketing strategy for someone, asking for only $2,500 to teach someone how to do it seemed very fair.

I lowered the class size because I wanted to be sure to give each student personal attention. I promoted this class to only my own e-mail list. I got five students, which meant I raised $12,500. Not bad for a month's work.

And yes, I bought the country estate. I'm writing this article from it.

You can do this, too. I've since taught several other people to teach their own e-classes. Yanik Silver, Paul Lemberg, John Harricharan, Tom Pauley, Blair Warren, Jillian Coleman—the list goes on an on. All of them made at least $10,000 on their first e-class. Tom Pauley, the last I heard, made over $112,000 teaching e-classes.

The lessons here? There are several:

1. *Intention rules.* You can float with the circumstances life brings you, or you can create you own direction and your own circumstances. It begins with a decision. What do you want? Decide. Choose. Declare.

2. *Break the model.* Just because others are selling their services for a song doesn't mean you have to, as well. Respect yourself. What are you worth?

3. *Go for something other than money.* Wanting my Z3 caused my mind to stretch in new ways to raise the money needed to get the car. If I were just going after money for money's sake, I might not be so bold in my ideas or my pricing. What do you *really* want?

4. *You can do this, too.* Just look at what you know that others would pay you to learn. Then turn it into an e-class, complete with lessons and assignments. After the class is over, you might even compile the material into a book, or a tape set, or . . . Think big! What would you teach if you had no fears?

5. *The spiritual is not separate from the material.* Since I've focused on money in this article, it might be easy to assume my focus was only on the dollar. Not so. I used spiritual principles—as outlined in my *Spiritual Marketing* (now called *The Attractor Factor*) book—to create wealth. Once you realize that the spiritual and material are two sides of the same coin, you are free to have happiness as well as cash. As it says on the dollar bill in your pocket, "In God we trust." Do you trust?

Finally, yes, I got my Z3. It's a 1999 Montreal Blue stunning piece of rolling beauty. I've never had so much fun driving in my life. In fact, I think I'll aim it up and down some Texas country roads right now. . . .

10

Five Things Every Internet Marketer Must Learn from Mail Order to Increase Profits Now

Jo Han Mok

Understanding that the Internet is another vehicle for direct response marketing can potentially make you rich! It's true. Not many people actually get it.

Information marketing has much in common with the old-school mail order business. In fact, many of the practices you see online today, such as two-page direct sales mini sites, mailing lists, and unique products, come directly from the mail order model. Every Internet marketer would benefit from studying the mail order industry. The basic marketing principles and practices employed by the industry translate naturally to the online environment.

The five core priorities of successful mail order companies parallel those of the online marketer: demographics, targeting, testing and tracking, up-selling, and customer follow-up. If you aren't focused on these key areas yet, read on to discover why you should be and what it will mean for your bottom line.

■ DEMOGRAPHICS

Demographic information provides an in-depth profile of your potential customer. There are two ways to acquire demographic information, and two separate motives for each method:

➤ Acquire data from consumer data mining companies such as MarketShare Online.

➤ Acquire data from your existing customer base.

The preferred source depends on your product development process and your current resources. Professionally gathered data allows you to survey the market and create highly targeted products. Rather than searching through keyword lists for potential niches, you can use demographic data to target specific classes of consumers based on their spending habits and disposable income. Your marketing strategy becomes much clearer with this data in hand. It allows you advance insight into your customers' interests, pricing points, and mind-sets. Now you have a baseline against which to test the effectiveness of your sales message.

You should also acquire as much demographic data as possible from your existing customer base and mailing list. Even when you possess the resources to pay for this information, you should still query your own customers. Why? Quite simply, you need to compare the profile of your existing customer base against your expected customer base. For example, if you sell a high-priced information product targeted towards small business owners, yet find that 50 percent of your list is composed of nonqualified tire-kickers, something is off with either your sales copy, your targeting, or both.

■ TARGETING

Here is a rule of thumb for you to memorize: Interest and need alone are not enough to generate a sale. This is a controversial statement, I know. Ask yourself the following question, though: How often have you found yourself interested in a product yet not purchased it? How often have you needed a product, yet not been able to afford it? The truth is that, in either case, despite your interest and your need, you were only marginally targeted when the offer was presented to you.

This subtle case points to the synergy between demographics and targeting. This is why mail order companies go to such great effort to acquire detailed information on the marketplace. Whether you send 100,000 pieces of mail or pay for 100,000 visitors to your web site, the goal is the same: Put the offer in front of the right people, at the right time. If you put the right offer in front of the right person at the wrong time, it's the same as no offer at all. It is untargeted.

■ TESTING AND TRACKING

You absolutely must test and track everything you do. You must track your pay-per-click campaigns, your newsletter mailings, and the paths taken by visitors to your web site. You must test your ad copy and your product pricing.

The testing and tracking phase of a marketing campaign marks the proving ground between demographics and targeting. Once you've acquired the data on your potential customer's behavior, you must track their actual behavior to find out if it matches the expected results.

Until you do this, you are really only guessing at what works. Every mail order company places a tracking code on their postcards. This allows them to zero in on the exact location, age, income, race, and marital status of responsive customers. When you first launch a product online, however, you are essentially blind to this information until you start tracking. But as you gather your data, you will discover which search engines and which newsletters pull the best. Over time, you will be able to match this up with deeper demographic data collected from your list and discover, at the very least, the age and income of your customers and which search engines they prefer.

Can you imagine knowing that men between the ages of 24 and 34, for example, prefer Google, or that stay-at-home mothers prefer Yahoo!? This type of data is priceless because it directs your targeting up front. This is the gold mine that awaits you when you devote careful attention to testing and tracking your campaigns.

■ UP-SELLING THROUGH ROBUST ORDER FORMS

Your order form can pull more profit through impulse purchases than you realize. Many Internet marketers seem to believe that one product should mean one simple order form. This is probably due to so many of us being self-taught. We copy what we've seen.

Have you ever stopped to examine a mail-in coupon or catalog form? Even when the offer ultimately focuses on one major product, the form still includes an up-sell and sometimes even a counteroffer. Look at these examples:

➤ "Yes! I'd like to order the Incredible Bikini Wax System for $49.95 today! Also, please include my 14-ounce bottle of Instant Soothing Moisturizer, a perfect complement to the Incredible Bikini Wax System and a steal at only $9.99." (Up-sell)

➤ "Yes, I'd like to subscribe to *Golfing Today*! Instead of the incredible offer of 12 issues for $14.99, I'd like to receive a full 52 issues a year for $29.95." (Counteroffer)

The reason for doing this, of course, is that the customer is already interested and already in a buying mind-set. You've done all the hard work to lead him to your site and you've enticed him with your sales letter. He's on the order page with credit card in hand. Why not use this moment to make a complementary offer? You can up-sell a related product of your own or of one of your joint venture partners for a profit split.

There's no risk in making the offer. The customer will either take you up on it or he won't. The important point here is that a robust order form, with additional offers, helps you squeeze out extra profit and cuts down the work of luring that customer back in the future to make additional purchases.

■ POST-SALE FOLLOW-UP

What happens to your customer after the sale? Take a page from the book of mail order secrets and follow up with that customer! If you've ever purchased anything through a catalog, you know what happens. You end up on their mailing list and continue to receive catalogs and other offers in the mail. In fact, you may receive so much mail from that company that you become irritated!

While I don't recommend going overboard with your mailings, I do recommend moving your customers to an announcement list or newsletter. You don't want a one-time shot with each individual. Rather, you want to build a lasting relationship. Your follow-up process should be designed with several goals in mind:

➤ To keep your name and brand in front of the customer.
➤ To build trust and credibility by sharing supporting material that adds value to the product.
➤ To maintain contact so that you can make additional offers in the future.

Customer follow-up is so important it can't be stressed enough. As a general rule, 80 percent of your sales will come from 20 percent of your customers. In other words, if someone purchases from you once, they are likely to purchase from you again, provided you take appropriate action and keep them connected to you.

Remember that your customers are human and may go through a variety of emotions after making a purchase. They may experience buyer's remorse. They may feel nervous about sharing their credit card information with you and then never hearing from you again. They may absolutely love you and your product and want to reach out for more information. You must tend to each of these variables in order to gain the customer's trust and appreciation, so follow up!

What will you do with the five lessons presented to you in this article? You have before you a nearly complete outline of a profitable business system for online marketing. Take these principles to heart and put them into practice. Know your market. Speak to your market. Connect to your market. I guarantee your profits will soar.

11

Printing Books Digitally

Dan Poynter

In self-publishing, you are both the book creator and book producer; you are the author and the publisher. You will need creative writing talent to become a published author and money to become a publisher. Of course, that is an oversimplification, but the point is that writing is a creative act and publishing is a business.

Anyone can be a publisher. The right to publish is guaranteed to you by the First Amendment of the Constitution of the United States. You do not have to get a license or register with anyone to publish a book. But it does cost money. In fact, one definition of *publisher* is the person or company that makes the book happen—the one who puts up the money.

Until recently, book printing was expensive. Nowadays you may sell out to a publisher or publish on your own. Getting your book published is what is important; how you break into print is not. A publisher will edit, design, typeset, lay out, proofread, print, and distribute your book. You may also perform these functions yourself or hire a book designer, deal with a book printer, and use a booktrade distributor.

■ DESIGN

Go to a bookstore and look on that shelf where your book will be. You will notice that each genre or category has a different design. For example, business books are usually in hardcover with a dust jacket and go for $29.95 or $34.95. Professional books—for doctors, lawyers, and accountants—are often in hardcover without a dust jacket and sell for much more. Children's books are oversize, are in full color, have exactly 32 pages, and if you put a dust jacket on them, they sell for five dollars more. And travel books are low-priced, on lightweight paper, and are tall and narrow so they will slip into a pocket or pack. Your book must look like the others on the shelf. Respect your category; this is not the area in which to be creative.

Select a book with a look you like. Check the color of the paper, the size of the type, the design of the book, and so on. Buy that book and use it as a model for yours. Someone else has invested a good deal of time and money to design a book that you like. Adapt that design for your own book.

■ TYPESETTING

You can typeset your book yourself with MS Word but your pages will look even better if you learn a page-layout program such as Page-Maker, InDesign, or Quark. Once you are done with the typesetting, you can convert the text file into a graphic file with Adobe Acrobat. Most of the files received by book printers today are in Adobe Acrobat portable document format (PDF).

■ PRINTING

Traditionally, the printing of the book has been the most expensive part of the publishing procedure. Due to the setup costs, printing is a numbers game. It used to be necessary to print at least 3,000 copies to achieve a reasonable per-unit cost. That meant a large printing

---

Types of Printing

POD (print on demand): Digital printing of one book at a time after it is ordered by a customer. POD is more expensive per unit because all the overhead must be charged to a single book.

PQN (print quantity needed): Digital printing of a small number of books for stock and promotion.

Press: Traditional ink-based printing requiring a minimum of 3,000 books to be economical.

---

bill. For example, if you were printing a 144-page softcover book measuring $5\frac{1}{4}$ by $8\frac{1}{4}$, your 3,000 copies might produce a print bill of $4,800. And you could not print fewer without the unit price going up—way up.

Now we have digital PQN (print quantity needed) printing: high-speed, computer-controlled, toner-based production. These machines print both sides of the paper at the same time and do not require a period for the ink to dry. Press setup time is virtually eliminated. The same 144-page book might cost out to 400 books for $1,200. The per-unit price is higher, but the invoice you have to write a check for is much lower.

The quality of the toner-based printing is actually better than with traditional press printing. There are no light and dark pages as in ink printing. Excellent color covers are usually done with the same toner process. The softcover or hardcover books look better than traditionally printed books. Delivery time for digitally printed books is normally five days from press proofs, and reprints take three to four days.

Writers have benefited from offset printing, computers, and the Internet. The next technological revolution is digital PQN printing. Digital book printing is faster, easier, and cheaper. Putting a lot of ink on paper is now just an option—a good one if there is large prepublication demand, such as advanced sales to bookstores and/or a sale to a book club. But there is no longer an automatic requirement to print 3,000 or more copies of your book on spec. So price is no longer an excuse for procrastinating on your book.

Here is a list of digital printers:

DeHart's Printing Services
Santa Clara, CA
Tel: 408-982-9118
http://www.DeHarts.com

Tri-State Litho
Kingston, NY
Tel: 914-331-7581
http://www.TriStateLitho.com

BooksJustBooks.com
New York, NY
Tel: 800-621-2556
http://BooksJustBooks.com

TPC Graphics
Haddonfield, NJ
Tel: 856-429-2858
TPClen-Pat@erols.com.

Fidlar Doubleday
Kalamazoo, MI
Tel: 800-632-2258
http://www.fidlardoubleday
   .com

Alexander's Digital Printing
Lindon, UT
Tel: 801-224-8666
http://www.Alexanders
   .com

Infinity Publishing
Haverford, PA
Tel: 610-520-2500
http://www.infinitypublishing
   .com

DigiNet Printing
Miami Lakes, FL
Tel: 305-825-9260
http://www.DigiNetPrinting
   .com

Morgan Printing and Publishing
Austin, TX
Tel: 512-459-5194
mprinting@austin.rr.com

Sir Speedy–Whittier
Whittier, CA
Tel: 562-698-7513
http://www.sswhittier.com

Sir Speedy–Scottsdale
Scottsdale, AZ
Tel: 480-947-7277, Ex 111
sstatt@SirSpeedy21120.com

Adibooks
Lowell, MA
Tel: 978-458-2345
http://www.adibooks.com

Dan Poynter has written more than 100 books since 1969 including Writing Nonfiction *and* The Self-Publishing Manual. *He is a past vice president of the Publishers Marketing Association, past-chair of NSA's Writer-Publisher PEG, and the founder of the PEG newsletter. Dan does not want you to die with a book still inside you. For more help on book writing, publishing, and promoting, see http://ParaPub.com.*

12

Ten Tips for Using E-Mail to Get News Coverage

Paul J. Krupin

Welcome to the world of electronic commerce. It's amazing but true—you can use e-mail to get publicity with the media. Articles can enhance your visibility, name recognition, reputation as an expert, and position in your industry.

But there are some tricks of the trade that are developing in this new marketing technique. E-mail PR is not hard to learn, and the benefits are substantial.

■ THE GOLDEN RULE: TARGET AND PERSONALIZE

Many years of Internet experience have shown me that publicists must abide by several essential rules in submitting e-mail to the media if they are to avoid the wrath of the recipients and maintain their reputation as a credible PR practitioner. Here are my 10 commandments for sending e-mail to the media.

1. *Think, think, think before you write.* Ask yourself why you are writing and what you are trying to accomplish by writing. Put yourself in the position of the person reading your message. As a busy media professional, what would you do upon receiving this message—publish it or toss it?

2. *Target narrowly and carefully.* Go for the quality contacts and not the quantity. Don't broadcast a query, news release, or announcement to irrelevant media. Pick out your target media carefully, based on the industry or readership of the specific media you are targeting. Study the media you are writing to. Write the way the editors write. Make it easy for them to use your submission.

3. *Keep it short.* Trim your e-mail message so that it fills one to three screens. Keep it three to four paragraphs tops. Don't try to sell the media your product. Do try to get their interest and elicit their request for more information.

4. *Keep the subject and content of your message relevant to your target.* It's got to be newsworthy and timely. The subject line should intrigue them enough to make them read your message. Present and propose problem-solving articles that advocate the benefits or techniques associated with a strategy, technique, product, or service. This article is an example.

5. If you are seeking publicity for a product or service, or want to get reviews for a new book or software, use a two-step approach: *Query with a hook and news angle before transmitting a news release or an article, or offer to send a review copy to those who request it.* Offer free review copies. To avoid angry replies and complaints about unsolicited e-mail, send a very brief e-mail requesting their permission to send them a release, before actually doing so.

6. *Tailor the submission to the media editorial style or content.* Go to a library, read the publication online, or write and ask for a free media kit and a sample copy of the magazine or journal. Study the style and content of the media. Then write the way they like it. Seek to develop a longer-term relationship as a regular contributor.

7. *Address each e-mail message separately to an individual media target.* Take your time and personalize each e-mail. Don't ever send to multiple addresses. It's the easiest way to get deleted without being read.

8. *Read, reread, and reread; write, rewrite, and rewrite, before you click to send.*

9. *Be brutally honest with yourself and with your media contacts.* Don't make claims about your product or service you can't prove.

10. *Follow up in a timely manner, with precision writing and professionalism.* Remember, there are real people at the receiving end. Your success with the media depends on your respecting the media and being courteous, plus your credibility, reputation, and performance.

Good luck and prosper. It is not hard to garner news coverage if you take your time and do a careful job. The benefits can be phenomenal. E-mail is a good way to make the most of limited funds. You can work locally, regionally, or nationally, and all you need is a computer with an Internet connection and e-mail.

You can and should use e-mail to get news coverage for your business, but you shouldn't rely on e-mail alone. When used together with conventional PR (mail, paper, phone, and fax), you get the maximum effect. Cultivate relationships with media by becoming known as a valuable contributor. If you give them what their readers want, they give you free publicity.

Paul J. Krupin can help you transmit your news releases to custom-targeted media lists via fax and e-mail. Contact him at IMEDIAFAX—the Internet to Media Fax Service—at 800-457-8746 or 509-545-2707, or on the Web at http://www.imediafax.com.

13

A Free Technique to Increase Visitors to Your Web Site

Bill Hibbler

A great way to drive traffic to your site is by giving testimonials for other people's products and services in your market. Most web sites will display your name and your site address below your testimonial. People see those testimonials and will often click on your link to see your site.

I have a testimonial on one of Corey Rudl's web sites, and it generates about 50 to 75 visitors a week and doesn't cost me a penny. That's not a huge amount of traffic, but that's just from a single testimonial.

Most hosting services provide you with statistics on how many visitors are coming to your site, and you can study those to see where visitors are coming from. If I place a testimonial and it brings me visitors, that will show up in my stats.

Randy Charach taught me an excellent technique for writing testimonials. Go to Amazon.com and look for best-selling books in the category that you wish to write a testimonial for. For each book, scan the user reviews. Above each review, look for the user rating (i.e., "18 out of 21 people found the following review helpful").

Pay particular attention to the reviews where 90 percent or more of the people agreed with the reviewer. Read the review carefully and pick up on the language the writer used. You'll want to model your own testimonials after these successful reviews.

Don't copy the review, but use similar words and tone for your own testimonials. Web site owners are more likely to use a testimonial that cites specific results rather than general praise. ". . . helped me increase my sales by 175 percent in one month!" is better than "Loved the course!"

Here's a tip for buying and selling e-books with resale rights. It takes just a few minutes to set this up, and it's free. Normally, when you buy an e-book with resale rights, you get the e-book and a ready-made sales letter in the form of a web page. You then add your order link and contact info to this page and use it on your web site or online auctions.

Most people just pass along the original generic web page when they resell the product. What I do is add my own testimonial (with my web address) to this page in an appropriate spot and include that page in my resale package. When customers resell the e-book, they put the modified page on their sites and auctions. This puts my name and web site address in front of their visitors. I get more traffic and it reinforces my credibility.

Bill Hibbler is the author of "The Rudl Report." Find out how to save (and make) big bucks on Corey Rudl products. Visit http://www.RudlReport.com.

14

Top 10 Ways to Add More Subscribers to Your List

Jo Han Mok

It's unbelievable. I personally know a few Internet marketers who

➤ Send ad after ad to their list without *any* content.

➤ Have no idea what they're recommending, as long as the affiliate commissions are attractive enough.

➤ Simply cut and paste ready-to-go ads without any modification to the copy.

➤ Do not communicate with their list at all.

And although learning about their malpractice was disturbing, I was even more shocked to know that these same guys were making a *ton* of money online.

Why? Simply because they had a monstrous quantity of quality, responsive subscribers who were Internet marketing junkies. A more precise term would be *rabid*. These guys are opportunity seekers who will do anything and everything under the sun to try to get rich on the Internet. They're completely irrational, and they're *hungry*. (Golfers, dentists, stamp collectors, antique collectors, musicians, and many other groups of people display similar irrational behavioral traits.)

Remember, a huge part of marketing success has to do with the receptivity of the prospect. So it's no wonder that those Internet marketing malpractitioners could get away with all those marketing sins and still wind up with a huge wad of cash in their back pockets. Not that I condone such malpractice, but I've got to tell you, it's the *list*. The magic's in the list.

Here are my top 10 ways to easily and almost effortlessly increase the size of your list. A lot of them tend to be overlooked, so do check off this list as you go along to see what else you can add to your arsenal of list-building tactics.

1. *Add more opt-in boxes in your sales letter.* Sprinkle more opt-in boxes into your sales letter. Ideally you should have one on top, one in the middle, one three-quarters of the way down, and one right at the bottom. This way, you have four chances of getting the opt-in.

2. *Increase the value of your subscriber bait.* People are not stupid. You need to prove that you're serious about creating a relationship with them and that it's worth their while to part with their e-mail address. Make sure you give away something valuable. This will stack the odds of you getting their e-mail address in your favor.

3. *Use a sig file for your e-zine.* It seems like pure common sense, but not everyone does it. Using a sig file to obtain a subscription is much easier than going straight for the sale of a product. Once you get your readers on your list, you can then proceed to build a relationship and sell them more products.

4. *Do joint ventures with other publishers.* I once took 10 minutes to set up a joint venture (JV) with a fellow e-zine publisher and managed to get a cool 1,885 subscribers. The JV cost me absolutely nothing, and yet these 1,885 additional subscribers have made me over thousands of dollars in sales and still continue to! If you can't find any JVs to participate in, *start* one!

5. *Get listed in e-zine directories.* Once again it sounds like common sense, but most people just don't do it! Go to Google, do a search for "e-zine directories," and you'll find many directories to submit your e-zine to, the majority of which are free.

6. *Use co-registrations.* Yes, if you're really lazy, you can actually buy subscribers. An example is http://www.listmedia.com. The caveat of using co-regs is that you'll need to make sure you have a good way of getting them to warm up and heighten their responsiveness.

7. *Write articles.* This is my personal favorite list-building tactic. Not all traffic is created equal. Subscribers gained from articles are more predisposed to what you have to offer because they practically opt in pre-sold. Plus, your credibility as an expert in your field has already been established, so the stage for your information facilitation has already been set.

8. *Use DHTML.* In addition to normal pop-ups and pop-unders, do use DHTML opt-in forms to collect e-mail addresses. That way, your opt-in box will not be blocked by pop-up blockers.

9. *Use an affiliate doubler.* I love this. It's a new Internet marketing technology that allows you to combine different web sites you wish to promote at a few clicks of the mouse. Check it out at http://www.affiliatedoubler.com. The list-building function will be apparent to you.

10. *Viral list building.* Free e-books are a great way of getting more subscribers and growing your online business, and with the right viral marketing approach, they could spread like wildfire and bring you primed and ready-to-buy subscribers on autopilot 24/7.

15

Fourteen Winning Methods to Sell Any Product or Service in a Down Economy

Robert W. Bly

Afraid the recession is here to stay a bit longer? If so, you're not alone. Many economists are predicting doom and gloom. And even if the economy hasn't hit rock bottom in your part of the country, it has slowed down significantly in many states.

But it doesn't take a recession or even a soft economy to create problems for your business. Every business has ups and downs. Even if things are going great guns right now, you need business-generating strategies that succeed when times are tough. Many businesspeople fear a recession or soft economy, reasoning that if the economy is poor, clients and customers will cut back on projects, stop spending, and—worse—sacrifice quality and buy only from low-priced vendors.

All of this is true—but only to a degree. An economic slowdown can be a problem for your business, or it can be an opportunity to gain new clients and boost your sales—if you know and have mastered the marketing and sales methods that work best in recessionary times.

What follows are 14 strategies that companies use to maintain and even increase their sales, while their competitors struggle to stay afloat. Apply these techniques to your own marketing and selling efforts during a recession, and you will survive—even prosper—while others struggle to get by.

■ REACTIVATE DORMANT ACCOUNTS

To reactivate a dormant account means contacting a past client or customer—someone you served at one time but are not actively working for now—and getting them to do business with you again.

The quickest and easiest way to do this is to sit down with your list of past clients or customers, call them, say hello, and see what's going on. Don't make this a hard-sell call. Tell them, "Hi, it's Jane. I'm calling just to check in and see how you're doing, since it's been a few months since we last spoke." Ask them what's new . . . how they're doing . . . what's going on with their business.

You don't have to ask for work directly, but when you end the conversation, you might say something like, "Well, it's been good talking with you. Keep in touch, and if there's anything I can ever help you with, don't hesitate to give me a call." This lets them know you are interested in working with them again, without putting the pressure on them to give you an order right then and there.

If you are uncomfortable phoning, you can send a letter, perhaps calling their attention to a recent article, literature on new products or services, or testimonial letters from your other accounts. This accomplishes essentially the same goal—to recontact the client or customer and remind them of your existence, products, services, and availability.

What kind of results will you get? It depends on whether you catch someone with an immediate or upcoming project with which they need help. On average, expect one order or assignment for every 10 calls you make.

Warning: Don't call up and say, "I'm not busy and need work

right now; do you have any assignments?" or "Things are slow; how about an order?" This is a terrible approach, for two reasons. First, the client or customer feels pressure, feels he has to come up with an excuse why he hasn't given you an order lately. This is uncomfortable and awkward for both of you. Second, it makes you seem desperate, and you do not want to seem hungry or needy.

In fact, a key goal of all of these 14 recession-fighting strategies is to make it seem that your purpose is to serve the client or customer better and more efficiently, not fill a gap in your slow work schedule. Always say you are calling to help *them*, and not, as is really the case, because you need the sale.

■ REACTIVATE OLD LEADS

If you're like me, here's how you handle inquiries: Someone calls. You send information. You call to follow up. They don't respond. You call again. After that, you give up and forget about them.

But believe it or not, many of those leads you simply gave up on can be turned into profitable business for you, with just a little extra sales effort. In fact, a study by Thomas Publishing Company reveals that most salespeople, regardless of the industry, give up too early. According to the study, 80 percent of sales to businesses are made on the fifth sales call, but only 10 percent of salespeople call beyond three times! So you have probably not followed up on leads diligently enough (for example, I almost never call more than twice), and the new business you need may already be right in your files.

The best way to reactivate these old sales leads is to call them. Ask whether they got your material, whether they have an immediate or future need, and what the status of that need is. This technique can be profitably used on prospects who have inquired within the last year or two. The best prospects, however, would probably be those who contacted you within the past six months. I find that one-quarter to one-half of the prospects will encourage you to send literature, and perhaps one or two out of ten will come through with an order.

■ HELP EXISTING CLIENTS CREATE NEW ASSIGNMENTS FOR YOU

Usually, my clients come to me with assignments they want me to handle for them. But if they don't, and I want to generate additional revenue, I will call them up and suggest marketing ideas they can use—ideas that they will ultimately ask me to implement for them. Normally, I encourage you not to give away your advice for free. But if business is slow, there's nothing wrong with tossing out a few quick ideas—things that may be obvious to you and you didn't spend a lot of time coming up with, but which will be extremely valuable to your client or customer.

For instance, when one of my clients introduced a new service, I immediately suggested a direct mail idea he liked, which resulted in a $2,500 copywriting assignment on the spot—a $2,500 assignment he would not have given me otherwise. So when things are slow, and the clients or customers aren't calling, you can call them and help them come up with assignments for you.

Key point: Obviously, your approach is "Here is an idea that can help you, Mr. Client (and by the way, I'd be happy to implement it for you)," *not* "Please give me an assignment so I can keep busy and make money."

■ GIVE A SUPERIOR LEVEL OF SERVICE

In a recession or during other times when business is slow, you want to do everything you can to hold on to your existing clients or customers—your bread-and-butter accounts.

The best way to hold on to your clients or customers is to please them. And the best way to please clients or customers is to give them not just their money's worth, but more than their money's worth. Now is the time to go the extra mile, give that little bit of extra service that can mean the difference between *dazzling* the client or customer and merely *satisfying* them.

The best protection against a downturn in new business is an active list of happy, satisfied clients or customers—people or firms who give you a steady stream of continuing assignments that pay the rent and feed the family. So cultivate your current clients or customers. Nurture them. Serve them well. Do *everything* in your power to make them happy and keep them satisfied with your product or service, so they keep coming back for more.

■ QUOTE REASONABLE, AFFORDABLE PRICES IN BIDS

If times are tough for you, they may be tough for others in your industry. Clients know this and may seek to take advantage by sending jobs out for multiple bids, where previously they might have come to you only. And if there's a recession, the cost of services or products will become more of a factor than it normally is; customers and prospects will be unusually price-sensitive. The solution is to bid competitively, but reasonably. If you are high-priced to begin with and you insist on getting top dollar, be prepared to lose out in some bidding situations.

How should you price your products or services during a slow period or a down economy? *Don't* instantly lower your prices to rock bottom. You may never be able to raise them again. Also, you don't necessarily have to reduce your prices, especially if your rate card or fee schedule presents a range of fees. You *should*, however, bid toward the middle or lower end of your published fee range, rather than at the maximum. For example, if you list $5,000 to $8,000 to write an annual report, quote a price of $5,000 or $6,000, not $8,000, to make sure you are not charging way more than other firms bidding on the job.

As a rule, during a recession you probably want to adjust your bids so they are 15 to 20 percent lower than what you would normally charge in a healthy economy. This gives your prospects the break they are looking for, shows fairness on your part, but does not cost you much in the long run.

Note: Do not tell clients or customers that the fee is a special reduced fee. Simply present it as your bid on the project. If customers and prospects sense you are cutting fees because you are losing assignments, they will take advantage and try to force your prices even lower. So keep your pricing tactics secret, and simply present the price as you normally would.

■ USE LOW-COST ADD-ONS TO GENERATE ADDITIONAL REVENUE

One way to generate some extra profitable business is to encourage clients or customers to add on to or expand existing assignments or purchases.

For instance, if one of my copywriting clients is doing an ad on a new product, chances are they need a press release also. I can upgrade the total project fee by offering to do both jobs for a package price. If my fee for the ad is $1,500, I may tell the client, "You also should send out a press release to all the publications in the field. I can write a press release while I do the ad for you; the additional cost is only $500." Frequently the client or customer will accept such a recommendation, and I get an assignment that is $2,000 instead of $1,500. And it's easy to do the small add-on project, since it uses the same basic background information and material provided for the main assignment.

This is an easy income-booster. Using this technique, you can increase the average dollar value of each project by 10 to 40 percent or more with *virtually* no extra sales effort. I often look for ways to add extra or ancillary assignments to the major assignment. It's good for me and good for my clients: I get more work, and they get a more complete service. Try it!

■ AVOID BEING A PRIMA DONNA

Let's face it. When you're busy, in demand, and have much more work than you can handle, it's great feeling. The tendency is to get a swelled head. My advice is don't. And why not? Because when things are slow—like now—it will come back to haunt you.

Nobody likes a prima donna. You don't, and neither do your clients or customers. You may put up with a contractor, doctor, or freelancer who's a prima donna because you feel they are the best source of service, and you know they're so in demand that you need them more than they need you. But you don't like it—in fact, you resent it—and you'll always be on the lookout for another supplier or professional to replace the prima donna.

Your customers feel the same way. And when the situation reverses—when things are slow for you, and the client or customer knows you need work from them, but they don't need you—they'll take revenge. And you'll be out.

The solution? Always, *always* act like a pro—like a helpful friend and consultant to your client or customer. Be useful, courteous, and accessible. Don't be a snob or act high-handed. If you give your clients or customers genuine reasons to like you, and you are always helpful to them, they'll stick with you—and that can make a big difference in your life when things get slow.

Remember, in a depressed economy, continuous business from ongoing, current clients or customers is what keeps you afloat. Make sure you have that business when you need it tomorrow by acting professionally and properly today.

■ POSTPONE PLANNED FEE INCREASES

A recession, depression, business downturn, or soft economy is not the appropriate time for you to increase your fees or prices, even if you feel you deserve it and that a raise is long overdue. During such a period, you should defer any planned fee increase announcements until later, and instead keep your fees at their current levels.

Note: Don't announce to your customers and prospects that you are holding the line on prices due to the recession and your desire to help them through it. Remember, even though you are feeling the effects of a soft economy, they may not be going through similar difficulties. Thus, your announcement would clue them in to the fact that you are in trouble. Some may then take advantage of your perceived need of business by haggling on price with you. So leave your fee schedule as is and continue with business as usual.

■ DOWNGRADE SLIGHTLY YOUR ACCEPTABLE CLIENT PROFILE

You have a set of written or mental guidelines that determine which clients or customers are desirable to you and which are not. During a depressed economy or personal business downturn, you may want to be more flexible in this area than you usually are. For instance, if you normally do business with Fortune 500 companies only, you may want to consider taking on assignments from smaller local firms—provided the pay is decent and their credit rating is good. Or, if you normally work only on major annual reports, you might consider knocking out some small quarterly reports to generate needed revenue.

This doesn't mean you throw your standards out the window and work for anyone who calls you. Far from it. Instead, you are simply readjusting your acceptable client or customer criteria during this temporary lull to accommodate a wider range of prospects and projects.

How far should you take this? It's up to you. If, for example, you normally have a minimum project fee of $1,000, you might accept $500 assignments, but you probably should stick by your guns and not take on $50 assignments.

■ PLAN AN AGGRESSIVE NEW-BUSINESS MARKETING CAMPAIGN

This strategy has two parts to it. The first part, which seems blatantly obvious, is that when things are slow, you increase the percentage of your time spent on marketing and prospecting for new business. For instance, if you usually devote 10 percent of your time and energy to marketing and sales when things are fairly busy, you might increase this to 25 percent when things are slow. During a lull in business, you need to make this extra effort to attract clients or customers, follow up on leads, and close sales.

The second part of the strategy may not be so obvious. It's this: To prevent a lull in business from ever happening in the first place, you should market consistently and aggressively all year long, every week—not just when you need the business. Planning an ongoing marketing campaign ensures a steady stream of new business leads. Marketing done today begins a selling cycle that will result in new business when you need it six months from now.

What types of marketing work best in a recession? Use a combination of result-getting direct marketing (direct response print ads, sales letters, self-mailers, postcard decks, special offers) plus low-cost/no-cost visibility-enhancing publicity techniques (press releases, articles, speeches, booklets, seminars, newsletters). Avoid costly image-building marketing such as large space ads, slick corporate brochures, expensive annual reports, and other marketing communications that drain your budget without producing measurable results.

■ REPACKAGE YOUR SERVICES

When you're busy, there's a whole group of prospects you probably turn away without a second thought. These are companies that are too small (read: too underbudgeted) to afford your product or service. But when things are slow, it pays to look for ways to generate revenue from this normally overlooked market segment. This is best done by repackaging your service or product line to accommodate smaller clients or customers and reduced budgets.

For instance, the client or customer who cannot afford to pay you $5,000 to write his direct mail package *can* afford to pay you $400 to critique a package he writes himself. He can also afford to pay you $100 an hour for your consultation services, take your full-day direct mail seminar for $200, or buy your book for $25.

Freelancers, consultants, and other service providers can repackage their expertise and services in a variety of formats, including hourly consultations, critiques, telephone consultations, newsletters, special reports, booklets, audiotapes, instruction manuals, books, seminars, and so on. Manufacturers and other product sellers can offer compact models, economy sizes, no-frills versions, special discounts, payment plans, and smaller minimum orders. These alternatives may not provide as complete a solution as the deluxe package, but they give the smaller client or customer the help he needs at the price he can afford. When the big companies are not giving you the big orders at the big prices, selling these alternatives to the less affluent segment of the market can put lots of extra dollars in your pocket.

■ ADD VALUE TO YOUR EXISTING SERVICE

In a recession or soft economy, clients or customers in all areas are more concerned with price than ever before. Actually, though, their real concern is making sure they get the best value for their dollar. You can win new accounts and retain existing clients or customers by enhancing your service and providing your clients or customers with more value for their dollar.

For instance, if you are selling a commodity item, you could add value by offering faster delivery than your competitors. Or you could offer a larger selection, more colors, more options, easier payment terms, or a better guarantee. There is no need to give away the store and promise an excessive amount of extra service. Just a little extra effort or service on your part will be perceived as a significant increase in value by the client or customer. And the extras you provide need not take a lot of time or cost a lot of money.

Always look for ways to give the client or customer not just their money's worth but *more* than their money's worth. These little extras always pay big dividends in client or customer goodwill and ongoing future assignments.

■ KEEP BUSY WITH ANCILLARY ASSIGNMENTS OR ACCOUNTS

A slow period in your business is a good time to busy yourself with other projects. Clean out your files. Develop a new marketing strategy. Make technical improvements to an existing product or service. Audit your customer support procedures. Revise your standard proposal or sales letter. Redesign your slide presentation. Or do any of a hundred things that need doing but never get done. Now you have the time, so do them. Don't waste the extra time moping. Instead, put it to good use. Be productive.

Another strategy is to take on ancillary assignments to fill in gaps in your work schedule. This keeps the money coming in until your regular business picks up again. For example, a carpenter who is normally busy with major home improvement projects saw business fall off during the slowdown of the early 1990s. His solution was to call old customers and offer to do odd jobs, small projects, and general handyman work to generate income until he got calls to do large remodeling jobs again.

■ BE POSITIVE

The most important thing about a slow period is not to be depressed by it. If you are depressed, prospects can sense your desperation and fear, and it has a negative effect on your dealings with them.

Remember that *everybody* in business has slow times; those who say they never do are liars. You are talented and successful. The lull is temporary. People will call you and hire you again.

Don't despair, and don't give up too soon. It is possible to have two, three, even four or more slow months. But if you follow the 14 strategies outlined in this chapter, you can turn things around and become busy and profitable once again.

Bob Bly is an independent copywriter and consultant specializing in business-to-business and direct marketing. He writes marketing plans, ads, brochures, direct mail packages, sales letters, and publicity materials for such clients as Associated Air Freight, Philadelphia National Bank, Value Rent-A-Car, Timeplex, Grumman, Edith Roman Associates, and EBI Medical Systems. He has taught copywriting at New York University and has presented sales and marketing seminars to numerous corporations, associations, and groups including the American Marketing Association, Business/Professional Advertising Association, Direct Marketing Creative Guild, Women's Direct Response Group, American Chemical Society, Publicity Club of New York, and the International Tile Exposition.

Mr. Bly is the author of 20 books, including How to Promote Your Own Business, Direct Mail Profits, The Copywriter's Handbook, *and* Create the Perfect Sales Piece. *His articles have appeared in such publications as* Cosmopolitan, Chemical Engineering, Computer Decisions, Business Marketing, New Jersey Monthly, Amtrak Express, *and* Direct Marketing. *He can be reached at his New Jersey office at 201-385-1220 or by e-mail at rwbly@bly.com.*

16

How to Find Your Exact Buyer on the World Wide Web

Dan Seidman

Marketing experts like Jay Conrad Levinson, Joe Sugarman, and Jay Abraham agree perfectly on one thing: The first thing you must do to promote your product or service is to identify your *exact* potential buyer. The following strategy is an excellent lead-generation system to discover the best people who are willing to spend money on you.

On the Web, it's fairly easy to locate watering holes where people interested in your topic gather to drink of the knowledge and experience the wisdom of their peers. Here are three strategic steps to take in your journey to sell on the Internet.

1. Set up a free e-mail account. Use this address only for this project. This keeps your existing e-mail account from becoming cluttered with your research. Get it free from a service like Hotmail.com or Yahoo.com.

2. Sign up for all e-zines that match your business or consumers' market, using this new e-mail account. This web site lists all the big and little e-zines: http://ezines.nettop20.com. You should also compile a list of keywords for your business type in order to search out all potential e-zines. In addition, go to the web sites of your clients and competitors and subscribe to their newsletters.

3. Read through these e-zines each week to find out which ones are quality newsletters, who is writing articles for them, and how large each subscriber list is.

Now that you have found them, what are some possible ways to get them to discover you and buy your product or service? Try these:

➤ Contact the best e-zines to ask if the publisher would review your web site or service.

➤ Post messages with your opinions and expertise to the subscribers.

➤ Write articles to share with the e-zine publishers. Remember, they have to produce new content for each issue. Your offer of help is greatly appreciated. A simple formula to construct an article is to describe a problem, make it worse (share the consequences of the trouble), then offer a solution (perhaps yours!). But don't blatantly promote your offering.

➤ A great way to leverage other writers who are already contributing to these e-zines is to e-mail them and comment on their articles. Be sure to mention that their writing caught your eye because your expertise is in that business area and you respect their insights. These can be turned into great strategic alliances. Of course, visit these writers' web sites and sign up for their e-zines.

➤ Consider placing ads in the best e-zines—if you can, contact other advertisers who said they make money from their ads.

Just begin to invest a little time communicating with others in your marketplace and you'll find a herd of buyers. And don't forget to stop and enjoy the chance to sip from others as well. You just might be someone else's buyer, too.

Target your market on the Web and you will sell more! Good hunting.

Dan Seidman is a speaker, author, and coach who manages the award-winning web site SalesAutopsy.com. His new book, The Death of 20th Century Selling: 50 Hilarious Sales Blunders and How You Can Profit from Them, *is available by calling toll-free 1-877-613-7355 or visiting www.salesautopsy.com/book.html. Dan can be reached at dan@sales autopsy.com. He is also available to speak at your sales conference or trade show on these very funny stories and innovative selling strategies.*

17

Seven-Day Plan for Making Instant Money Online

Yanik Silver

In just seven days you can be making money by following this simple, day-by-day, step-by-step plan.

■ DAY 1

Find an affiliate program to match these criteria:

➤ Subject you are immensely interested in.
➤ Proven sales process.
➤ High payout (ideal if it is recurring or if you get paid on additional back-end products).
➤ Reputable company.

Sign up for the affiliate program.

Buy the product using your new affiliate ID number. Cost: product cost less affiliate commission.

■ DAY 2

Sign up for an autoresponder service. I recommend http://auto responder2.yanikrecommends.com because you'll be building a big list, and this company lets you broadcast for free and use tracking. You'll soon see why all that's important. Cost: $19.95/month.

Write two ads. Write a classified ad for the affiliate product (5 to 10 lines) and also write a solo e-zine ad (this is a long ad—more like a small sales letter). Some affiliate programs have samples for you. Ours does (see www.surefiremarketing.com/affiliate/). It's ideal if you write your own—however, it's not necessary. When writing your ad, be sure to make the call to action your new autoresponder address and not just the affiliate link for your new program. This is key because you want to capture the names of interested prospects and follow up with them.

Write three follow-up sequences for your autoresponder. The first one should simply give people highlights of the product you recommend and then give your affiliate link. The next two follow-ups can simply be reminders for people to check out your affiliate recommendation. Optional: If you really want to start making sales, you should give away a special free bonus, available only from you, that people would e-mail you to get, with verification they ordered through your link. This is powerful. You can give away free books, software, and so forth.

■ DAY 3

Go to several e-zine directories to find good places to advertise. An optional paid e-zine directory, such as www.lifestylespub.com

/wow, will set you back $39.95. Here are some other possible places to look:

➤ EzineSeek: http://www.ezineseek.com

➤ eZINESearch: http://www.ezinesearch.com

➤ E-ZineZ: http://www.e-zinez.com

➤ BestEzines: http://www.bestezines.com

Get rate cards, look at sample issues if possible, and also subscribe to any you are thinking about. Which brings me to an important point: You probably already get several e-zines that accept advertising, since you're already interested in your subject matter. If that's the case, look through your in-box and see what kind of e-zines you read. Remember, you want e-zines with good strong content, not something people just delete. And if you're a subscriber you'll know firsthand how substantial they are.

Depending on your budget, go with either a classified ad or a stand-alone ad if available. Use your autoresponder's tracking code for each separate ad you run (i.e., nameofautoresponder.code@aweber.com). Also, if the affiliate program can do tracking, you can use that same code in your follow-up efforts. Or simply sign up for several affiliate accounts to track different ads. It's critically important to know whether you made or lost money.

Book at least one ad.

■ DAY 4

Go back to your bookmarks and see which discussion groups you may already go to. Start there and think about how you will contribute to the discussion going on (notice I didn't say "post your ad"). Be on the lookout for questions posted that you can answer. As you answer the questions, usually each board gives you the opportunity to post a link. That's where you post your affiliate link.

Be careful that you get a feel for discussion boards before posting, because you do not want to spam a board with blatant advertising.

■ DAY 5

If your ad has already run, you may start to see an affiliate commission come in. That's great and encouraging, but the real money is going to be in repeat sales to your newly created list of people who triggered your autoresponder.

If you're starting to see some money come in, please, please reinvest that. Don't spend it! Look for additional places to put e-zine advertising. You should consider multiple ads, or upgrading from a classified ad to a solo ad.

■ DAY 6

Add two or four more messages to your autoresponder sequence, spaced about 10 days apart. These should be additional endorsements for other products. Also, you should add one or two sequences of content. These could be free articles with your affiliate link.

■ DAY 7

By now you should have a list of a couple hundred prospects. You should start researching additional products that you can endorse or buy rights to. Then you will send out one e-mail blast and direct them to your site, which you can start building now.

Just 29 years old, Yanik Silver is recognized as the leading expert on creating automatic, moneymaking web sites—and he's only been online full-time since February 2000! He is the author and publisher of several best-selling marketing books and tools, including these:

> ➤ *www.InstantSalesLetters.com*
> ➤ *www.InstantInternetProfits.com*

➤ *www.InstantMarketingToolbox.com*
➤ *www.33daystoonlineprofits.com*
➤ *www.WebCopySecrets.com*

Yanik specializes in creating powerful systems and resources for entrepreneurs to enhance their businesses. When away from the office Yanik enjoys beach volleyball, ice hockey, skiing, and working on his terrible golf game.

18

Avoiding the Delete Button: Make Your E-Mail Campaign Pay Off

Diane Hughes

Success is measured not by what you do for yourself, but what you do for another person's self-interest.

—Diane Hughes

Have you noticed? It's becoming harder and harder to get a good response out of e-mail campaigns. Why? The more popular an advertising method becomes, the more overused it gets. When that happens, customers develop an immunity. They are so overwhelmed by the dozens, or even hundreds, of e-mails that pop into their in-boxes that they simply hit the delete button without even giving it a second thought.

So how do we, as Internet marketers, battle their complacency? There are several ways that have been proven to increase customer response. I'll share six with you here. I'll assume that you already have a customer-focused, sales-oriented web site, and that your offer is a solid one that shows value.

1. *Use short, concise subject lines.* While personalization has been shown to increase response rate, several things have been proven to decrease it. Long subject lines are one. Try to keep yours at 40 characters or less. Why? Many e-mail programs cut off longer subject lines. Also, avoid phrases that sound like hype. The more personal you are, the better. Exclamation points, the word *free*, and other trigger words such as *boost* and *skyrocket* are a sure ticket to the delete file.

2. *K.I.S.S.* Remember this acronym? "Keep it simple, stupid." It applies to e-mails, too. Don't piddle around. Get your benefits in front of the reader immediately. Likewise, shorter e-mails have proven to outperform longer ones. It is doubtful that you'll actually sell to anyone from your e-mail ad—rather, aim to pique readers' interest, and get them to click to your site.

3. *Timing is everything.* Didn't think that mattered? Oh, it does! The day of the week and the time of day play a significant role in how effective your campaign is. For example, almost everyone is in a rush in the morning hours, which means there's a greater chance that they will delete any e-mail they do not absolutely have to read. Take note of your target customers' typical schedule, and send your e-mails during their off times.

4. *Give a deadline.* One simple instruction to act before a certain date can make or break your success. Don't neglect this vital element!

5. *Consider HTML.* These days, most e-mail programs are HTML compatible. In fact, over 90 percent of customers can receive HTML e-mails. Color—whether in print or on the Web—always increases readability, if done tastefully. Consider having your e-mail converted to HTML to make it stand out in the sea of plain-text messages.

6. *Give it a break.* Rather than writing long paragraphs (even a three-sentence paragraph formatted at 65 characters per line looks long), write in short one- or two-sentence blips. This is easier on the eyes of the reader and doesn't take nearly as long to digest.

The competition for your customer's attention is growing greater by the day. Refining your e-mail campaign can help you avoid the delete button and reap greater profits.

Diane Hughes is an accomplished Internet entrepreneur and editor of the popular ProBizTips Newsletter. Learn more about Diane and her success in helping many start a home business and make money from home, by visiting http://viralmarketzone.com/diane.

19

Five Simple Ways to Increase Your Web Site Conversion

Jo Han Mok

Does it really matter how many visitors your web site receives? Let me share an inside joke among top gun Internet marketers. HITS: How Idiots Track Sales.

Fact: It's not about raw hits. It's about getting targeted traffic and converting them from browsers to buyers. The truth is, if your web site does a bad job of that, then it really doesn't matter how many hits a month you get, does it? Conversely, if you sell a $49 product and you can convert 15 percent of your visitors, you'll have a visitor value of $7.35! Imagine each visitor being worth $7.35 to you!

If that's the case, then you really don't need that much traffic going to your web site. Think about it: If you only get 1,000 visitors, you'll net a cool $7,350 in profits! And anyone who's been in the business long enough will tell you that with the right advertising, you can easily get 1,000 targeted visitors at the drop of a hat.

So it's not the numbers. It's about qualified numbers and what you do with them! Here are five simple ways you can increase your web site conversion rates.

■ GRAB 'EM BY THE THROAT

The first thing your web site needs is a killer headline that will stop readers dead in their tracks. As amazing as it sounds, a killer headline can potentially increase your response by up to 1,700 percent by tomorrow afternoon. To quote David Ogilvy, five times as many people read the headline as they do the body copy.

Here are some tips to help you craft that killer headline better and faster:

> ➤ Craft your headline based on the frustration of your target market. What keeps them awake at night? If you know exactly what makes them tick, you can create a headline that goes straight for the jugular.

> ➤ Use quotation marks around your headlines. Quotation marks, as tested by masters like Ted Nicholas and Gary Halbert, among many, actually heighten response rates.

> ➤ When suffering from writer's block, it's usually hard to go wrong with a how-to type of headline.

■ MAKE 'EM CURIOUS

Want to know how curiosity works? People simply cannot stand having a secret kept from them. This psychological law is one of the most powerful driving forces behind many of the most successful copywriting controls ever.

You can leverage this law to compel your prospect to continue reading your copy. It's like sucking your reader in with a monstrous vacuum cleaner. And if you use this law, it doesn't matter which school of thought you subscribe to: "The more you tell the more you sell" or "The more they read the more they need." It'll work for you both ways.

The key to making this work is this: Your reader must think that there is *something* preventing them from getting the results they should be getting, and that the sales letter they're reading is the missing link.

■ SHOCK 'EM

Would you be interested in learning something that you already know? Not very likely.

Controversy sells. It's cliche but it's true. If your web site copy reveals why your readers are wrong about something they have always taken for granted was right, you'll radically increase your readership, guaranteed! It's the very same reason that people like tabloids.

Let me give you an example. If I have a headline that says "Shocking! New Medical Study Reveals That Vitamin C Causes Cancer!" would you be interested in reading the copy? Pick up a copy of the *Enquirer*, some women's magazines, and *Reader's Digest*. There's a lot that you can learn from such publications to increase your web site conversion rates.

■ INVOLVE 'EM

People absorb information through different modalities. There are three main types of modalities:

1. Visual
2. Auditory
3. Kinesthetic

Most people learn through mixed modalities, although they usually tend to slant towards a particular one.

Visual people like to see stuff. Such people usually have no problems reading web site copy and are usually very receptive to hypnotic triggers like "Imagine this . . . ," "Picture this . . . ," or "See yourself . . ."

Auditory people like to hear stuff. With all the new web site audio streaming technology, you can easily get started with a product like Audio Generator or Sonic Memo and start getting your web site to talk. Video would appeal to both the visual and audial groups, and the technology is now available to make this a viable option.

Kinesthetic people like to have a hold on stuff. They "grasp" things easily and usually like to learn "hands on." You can ask them questions in your body copy, add check boxes that they can check off as they go along, and incorporate interactive quizzes to capture their attention.

The bottom line: Offer a multimedia experience. This will enhance the stickiness of your site.

■ MAKE 'EM LOOK

Not many people talk about this, but the look of your web site is important if you're serious about increasing your conversion rates. Here are some things to consider:

➤ Fonts: Tahoma for headlines and Arial for body copy are usually a very good combination. Occasionally, Courier and Verdana work as well.

➤ Cosmetics: Are you bolding, italicizing, and highlighting?

➤ Tables: Tabling your testimonials and bullets makes your web copy look neater and easier to read.

➤ Colors: The colors you choose for your body copy are also very important. You can be aesthetic and have a color scheme but it should increase readership. Otherwise it's completely redundant and useless. Usually you'll want to have a dark background, so that the eyes of your prospect are centered on the body copy because of the contrast that's going on.

If it increases readership, do it! As you can see, these web site conversion strategies cost almost next to nothing, save for some time. But is that time spent well worth it? Your increased sales will be the judge.

20

Making Easy Money Online

Terri Levine

Whether you operate your own business on or off the Web, many of the once accepted methods of attracting new customers are no longer valid. Pop-ups annoy people and, rather than attract them to your offers, will turn them away in droves. You cannot send marketing e-mails out to just anybody anymore because this is spam, and it is now so out of control that specific software programs are being used by more and more people to block such messages.

Legitimate methods of making money do exist, however, and one of the easiest for the beginner is to join affiliate programs. You can become an affiliate of almost any business these days, and with many businesses now paying up to 50 percent on any products you sell, this really is easy money.

You can sell anything from books to loans, insurance, clothing, jewelry, and so forth, by simply using the affiliate link they give you in your e-mail signature, or by having a link to your web site so that when people leave your site, your affiliate company's web site will automatically appear next.

If you are part of a chat group, you can mention your affiliate product there. As long as it does not read like an advertisement or spam, you should be able to get away with it. The best way is simply to place it beneath your name as part of your e-mail signature, with an attractive description that will entice people to click on the link. You can also use your newsletter, if you have one.

The one thing you cannot and should not do is send out a mass e-mail to anyone and everyone, trying to sell your products. This will get you into trouble and blacklisted as a spammer. Many companies who operate affiliate programs specify they do not tolerate this, and you will lose your affiliate membership.

If you are looking for affiliate programs to join, try typing the words "affiliate program" into your Web browser search area; or, if there are specific companies with whom you'd like to establish an affiliate membership, go to their web site and have a look. Most companies provide a specific link or sign-up facility for affiliate purposes, but if you cannot find anything, try e-mailing them to ask.

You can have as many affiliate memberships as you like. Of course, you can't advertise all of them at once, but you can rotate them, giving them all an equal airing. You may find some work better than others. It costs you nothing to become an affiliate, but the benefits are there for those who know how to make the most of them without breaking any laws or spam regulations.

Terri Levine, MCC, PCC, MS, CCC-SLP, is the president of Comprehensive Coaching U—The Professional's Coach Training Program; a popular master certified personal and business coach; public speaker; and author of three best-sellers: Work Yourself Happy, Coaching for an Extraordinary Life, *and* Create Your Ideal Body. *She can be contacted via the web site http://www.ComprehensiveCoachingU.com or by telephone: 215-699-4949.*

21

Team Up with Great People

Bob Serling

My tip is so simple, it will almost sound obvious. It's extremely powerful, yet very few people ever take full advantage of this technique—if they even use it at all.

My advice is this: Surround yourself with the best people you can find. Look for people who are smarter, better, or faster at what you want to do than you are. Hire them, partner with them, co-market with them, and harness the power of teamwork every way you possibly can.

Think you can't get great people—even experts in their fields or well known celebrities—to work with you? You can. All you have to do is ask. Now, I'm not naively suggesting that everyone you ask will work with you, but as long as you make your request in a professional and compelling manner, many will.

Here is an example of how I'm using this technique in my own businesses. In my product development business, when I wanted to sell a toy to a major toy manufacturer, I teamed up with one of the top names in that industry to get the deal done in record time. This top expert had never heard of me, but I made a professional presentation to him, offered a full third of the revenue for making a couple of key introductions, and the deal was made. The results? We'll reap handsome royalties for many years to come.

Here's another example. My new e-zine, *Copy Doctor—The Cure for Ailing Response*, features 12 world-class copywriters doing free critiques of subscribers' actual marketing pieces. At first, I was going to do the critiques alone. But I quickly recognized that it would be much more powerful to have a team of the best copywriters in the world working with me to create copywriting breakthroughs for my subscribers. The appeal is far stronger than me working alone. Plus, because each of the team members gets constant exposure to my subscribers, it's a win-win deal for everyone.

Try this technique in your own business. I guarantee you're going to love the results.

Bob Serling is an editor and the founder of Copy Doctor. Tired of lukewarm response to your marketing? Team up with 12 world-class copywriters to get the results you've always dreamed of. Complete details are at www.Copy-Doctor.com.

22

Help Your Business with a Free E-zine

Shel Horowitz

Wouldn't you like an easy way to do these things?

- ➤ Capture e-mail addresses of one-time visitors to your web site—prospects who may otherwise never become customers.
- ➤ Build loyalty and credibility—and sales!—among your prospects.
- ➤ Develop an audience that eagerly awaits your special offers.
- ➤ Get crucial market research without having to pay for it.
- ➤ Provide an ongoing source of free content for your web site—and for the search engines.
- ➤ Put your message in front of large, new audiences—without spending a penny.
- ➤ Create a revenue stream through ads and product/service sales, at no cost to you.

You can do all these things at once—by starting your own e-zine. Once you build critical mass, you can reach new audiences by recycling your articles onto other people's sites and newsletters, and by exchanging ads with other publishers. You also can use your subscribers as a resource—to grow your list, to give you feedback on product titles and covers, and much more. I even hired my wonderful assistant by posting my needs in my e-zine.

It usually takes me only about half an hour to write each actual tip, and about as long again to deal with the formatting, ad placement, routine information, and so forth. In other words, it's not a big deal in terms of my time. In fact, I wrote a four-part series on e-mail marketing, January to April, in one sitting at a doctor's waiting room, accompanying my injured son through a medical exam and X-ray.

I strongly recommend that you do at least one e-zine, make it as good and useful as you can, and see what happens.

Shel Horowitz, owner of http://www.frugalmarketing.com, has been publishing Shel Horowitz's Monthly Frugal Marketing Tips *every month since May 1997. A copywriter and marketing consultant specializing in low-cost, high-ROI methods, he is the author of four marketing books. His two most recent are* Principled Profit: Marketing That Puts People First *and* Grassroots Marketing: Getting Noticed in a Noisy World.

23

The Secret to Forming Profitable Joint Ventures

Barry Boswell

Forming joint venture arrangements does not have to be complicated if you follow a few simple steps. This chapter will give you a quick method to get you going.

The basic premise you need to understand is simply this: If you target a prospect who is a likely candidate for your offer, the odds are very high that he or she will consider your proposal. Notice that I did not say *accept* your proposal; I said *consider* your proposal. Your first objective should be to get your prospective partner to listen to you. The more compatible your product or service is with your prospect and their customer base, the better the odds that your deal will be accepted.

Let's look at how you should begin. The first step is to determine what you are looking to accomplish and what you can offer your prospect. Then select an ideal prospect or candidate who can benefit the most from what you have to offer. The final step is to craft a proposal to your prospect that provides as little downside risk as possible. In other words, structure your offer in a win-win proposal, preferably with you assuming most if not all of the risk. Your odds for acceptance

increase as you more closely match your ideal prospect to your offer—
and decrease the risk that your partner would have to assume.

It is also preferable that your partner do as little work as necessary when structuring a joint venture. The more work that person
has to do to implement the arrangement, the less the chance that he
or she will accept your proposal. Try to make it as simple as possible
to implement.

Let me demonstrate the process using an example of some deals
that I recently put together. As a distributor for a manufacturer of a
line of anti-aging nutritional supplements, I have an affiliate program.
Because of this, I recently began a campaign to actively recruit affiliate
partners. The first step was to assess what benefits I could offer my
prospective partners. I determined that I could offer the following
benefits:

➤ A weekly newsletter, in which any referrals would be permanently tagged to my partner.

➤ Products that have a reorder rate of slightly over 80 percent.

➤ Reports in PDF format that could be personalized for my affiliate.

➤ Lifetime tracking of any traffic.

➤ A monthly continuity program so that customers could have
   their products on autoship, thereby assuring a continuous income stream to my affiliate partners.

The second step was to determine who could benefit the most
from what I had to offer. I decided that an e-book publisher of a
health or diet topic was my most ideal candidate. Furthermore, I
could approach these potential partners with different scenarios depending upon what systems they had in place. For example, if they
did not have their own newsletter, they could brand mine on their site
with an exit pop-up box. They could give their visitors and customers
a report branded with their affiliate link, offering them viral possibilities. Or the report could be positioned as a bonus to their product to
help them sell more of their own product. These e-book publishers
would now have the opportunity to turn a one-time sale into an ongoing source of revenue and offer their customer an additional bonus
at the same time.

By focusing on how I can add value to my partner, I can at least get webmasters to listen to my proposal—and, more importantly, to join my growing list of affiliates. You can apply this logic to many situations, even if you don't have an e-commerce business. Let me show you how.

Let's say you come across a product that sells quite well off-line. You approach the owner with an offer to market it online. Now you determine who online has the ideal customer for that product, along with enough traffic to support the venture.

You can structure a commission for yourself. The webmaster promoting the product earns additional income by selling the product. You can get a decent idea of the traffic a site gets by visiting Alexa (www.alexa.com). There is also an incredible software package available that will tell you the number of links that a site has. This information is indispensable for doing research of this nature. You can see it at http://scamfreezone.com/t.cgi?a=191230&e=/spider.

I hope you use this information to structure many ethical and profitable relationships.

Barry Boswell is an active online marketer, specializing in forming wildly profitable and mutually beneficial relationships. Discover his unique system at http://HealthyBody.Xtend-Life.com. For additional resources and information on joint ventures and how to structure them, send an e-mail to JointVentures@ProReply.com and the information will be forwarded immediately.

24

Simple Tips
with a Dash of
Common Sense

Cathy Stucker

You have a web site. It looks nice. It's packed with lots of good information about your business, your products, your services. But you realize it's not visible on the Web—traffic to the site is minimal, and what traffic you receive is not producing a real result.

You had hoped your web site would produce more calls for your service, more leads for your salespeople, or at least more downloads of your free newsletter, e-book, or white paper. You are thinking, what's the deal? Where is all the traffic and why am I not getting any leads, sales, or telephone calls?

Before you go out and drop a small fortune on a graphics designer to update your site or an SEO firm to analyze your HTML code, let's start simple.

■ "DON'T MAKE ME THINK"

It's sage advice from Steve Krug's book of the same title, especially when you are reminded the average time spent by a new visitor at a web site is typically less then 30 seconds. The suggestions I give you are not going to turn your site into a traffic monster or cash generator, but keeping Steve's mantra in mind is just common sense. People like doing business with others who consistently show common sense making it it easy to do business with them.

■ ASK FOR WHAT YOU WANT

Let your first-time visitors know what you want. If your most-wanted result from search engine traffic is to call you—which is typical of a service-oriented site—ask them to call you. Yes, really ask for what you want—professionally, of course—rather than beating around bush and making the visitor wander around the site aimlessly.

■ BE CLEAR ABOUT HOW TO CONTACT YOU

Give the visitor specific information as to when you are available. For example, Monday through Friday, 10 A.M. to 2 P.M. CST—and for goodness sake, include your time zone. If you prefer e-mail only, say that. Be specific.

Make all your contact information visible, especially on your home page. Find a way in your page design to put all this information toward the top of the page, not the very bottom.

■ BE CREATIVE AND KEEP SELLING EVERYWHERE

Remember to make your "Contact Us" or "About Us" page a selling opportunity. It's very likely someone will find you in the search engines and all they get is a contact page with phone number and address. Make sure you've included some kind of selling statement about your products and services—something unique that catches their attention. Draw them into your site. Yes, this holds true for all your pages.

■ GIVE A GIFT—MAKE IT EASY

I went to Starbucks the other morning and they had a neat stack of little squares of coffee cake they were giving away. I left the store spending twice what I had planned, and full—I had eaten three pieces, all free. I'm a regular now.

Offer something of real value to your first-time visitors. Make it easy for them to get it, rather than having to fill out 15 fields of red-asterisk-dotted *required* fields. Offer something for free that requires nothing from the user. Then step them into something of more value that requires only a first name and e-mail address. You'll end up with a lot more traffic, e-mail, and conversions over time, because people will come back to give back.

■ BRING IT ALL TOGETHER IN ALL YOUR E-MAILS

Ask for what you want. Tell who you are and how to get ahold of you, and give a gift. You can do this every day in all your e-mails to drive traffic to your site. Okay, you know about this, but are you doing it—all the time?

Here is an example I created for a client:

Experience the beauty of faux finishing and increase your opportunity for professional growth. Sign up today at www .viginistudios.com/faux-finishing-workshops.htm.

Have a question? Call now! Toll-free: 877-977-3289 Monday– Friday 9–5 CST, or e-mail us at faux-finishing@viginistudios .com for free online course.

And here's another example of bringing it all together:

Tom Parish is a left-brain/right-brain guy who applies his creativity to making web sites more visible to the naked eye, and more compelling for insane sales.

So call me Monday–Friday 1–4 P.M. CST and receive a free consultation. No question too small or too large to ask, so don't be shy.

Tom@4webresults.com is an Austin SEO and Web marketing consultant.

■ WRITE A BOOK AND GET IT ON AMAZON

Write a book and get it on Amazon.com and you will bring the world to your door. Think you can't write a whole book? Think you can't find a publisher or afford to self-publish? Think again.

I started my publishing company with $200 and made a profit my first day in business. (You can read the whole story at http://www.SellingBooks.com.) A few years later, I decided to try selling one of my books on Amazon. These early books were comb-bound manuals, not the perfect bound books you see in bookstores; however, I'd had a lot of success with my little comb-bound books, and decided I was ready for Amazon.

The Advantage Program allowed me to get up and running quickly. Amazon takes a large percentage of the sales price, but soon I was getting a nice check every month from them. I knew it was time to move up from my comb-bound books to a "real" book, and I began preparing the fifth edition of *The Mystery Shopper's Manual*. That's when the call came.

A writer for *Woman's Day* magazine was preparing a story that included mystery shopping. She found my book (yes, that little comb-bound thing) on Amazon and called to interview me as an expert on mystery shopping. The article, mentioning my book and my web site, appeared just as the fifth edition was coming off the press. In just days I sold enough books through my web site to pay for the entire print run of more than 5,000 books.

Journalists often turn to Amazon.com when they are looking for experts. If you have written a book, you are an expert. So write a book and get it listed on Amazon. You will lead media and customers to you and generate fame and fortune you may not have imagined.

That's my phone—gotta go. It might be Oprah!

Cathy Stucker has lots of great ideas to help you attract customers and make yourself famous. Get a free tip every week in Bright Ideas! *Sign up for your free subscription at http://www.IdeaLady.com/. And learn more about marketing, publishing, and creating your expert reputation, there and at http://www.SellingBooks.com/.*

25

How to Create Your Own Profitable Book in One Hour

Joe Vitale and Jim Edwards

Many years ago a stunning blonde woman stopped me (Joe) dead in my tracks at a trade show in Chicago for publishers. She thought I was a book reviewer, and she was dead set on getting all living book reviewers to see her client's new book. I was next in line. I'm glad I didn't run.

As it turned out, her client had put together a collection of inspiring quotes. I don't recall his name or the book's title, but I do vividly remember that woman and what she told me. "We've sold 100,000 copies of the book so far," she announced to me.

Now stop and think about this. What you are about to realize can help you became a profitable author in as little as one hour—or even less.

That woman's client was selling a book *he didn't write*. His book was a collection of quotes by other people. He may or may not have tossed a quote by himself in there, too. The point is, he put together an entire book by not writing a single word himself. And yet he not only is considered the author of the book, but his perky salesperson is out there selling it like it's the next *Harry Potter*!

I just looked on Amazon and found 539 books of quotations listed. Pretty impressive for books that aren't so much written as they are collected.

The point here is that you can create your own profitable book in far less time than you think. You can write your own book in less than seven days. You write a short book in an afternoon. And you collect quotes on any theme you might imagine and have it done tonight.

What are you waiting for?

Joe Vitale and Jim Edwards are the authors of Learn How to Write and Publish Your Own Outrageously Profitable eBook in as Little as 7 Days . . . Even If You Can't Write, Can't Type, and Failed High School English Class! *See http://www.7dayebook.com.*

26

Niche Marketing Secrets

Rufina James
and
Bart Baggett

■ KNOW YOUR MARKET FIRST

The first step in making tons of money on the Internet is to know WHO you are selling to and find out what they want. Then just give it to them. Your product is secondary to the market. Give people what they want and you'll always make money.

If your web site is seen by the wrong people, it will fail no matter how good it is. Your *market* will determine what you sell and how you sell it. For example, if you live in a community where people eat only Chinese food, your hot dog stand will fail—even if you have the best hot dogs in the world. But if you are selling directions to the nearest well and you're surrounded by hundreds of very thirsty people, you'll be flooded with customers. Similarly, if 65,000 people search for the word *parrot* on the Internet every month, and you show them your web site which sells a course about teaching parrots how to talk, then you'll have an easy time making sales. You would have a very difficult time selling your parrot course to a group of people who were searching for information about fishing.

So instead of placing your focus on "what's the ideal product?" spend your time looking for an ideal market. Once you find the ideal market, ask them what they want and give it to them.

■ FINDING A HUNGRY MARKET

When you're looking for a group of people to sell to, check for these three must-have qualities:

1. They must have an irrational passion about a certain hobby, problem, or topic. You want these people to be willing to spend any amount of money to fuel their passion and desire. For example, many golfers will buy every single golf gizmo in the world if they think it'll take a point off their score. Some balding men will spend thousands to get their hair back.

2. They must have money. There is no point in selling to people who can't buy. A car nut who is broke cannot buy your Ferrari no matter how much he loves it.

3. They must be great in number and easily reached. If you have only a few people to sell to, or you cannot find an easy way to market to them, then your business will dry up.

When you find a group like this and you offer them something that satisfies their passion and desire, then making sales is relatively easy. Even if your web site isn't perfect, even if your sales letter isn't perfect, and even if you have typos everywhere, you'll still make sales if you're selling something that an ideal market wants. If you were on fire, chances are you'd buy a bucket of water from just about anybody—even if he was dressed like a bum, smelled bad, and had the rustiest bucket you'd ever seen.

■ WHERE TO LOOK FOR YOUR IDEAL MARKET

There are plenty of great places to find a hungry market. Here are two:

1. *Your local bookstore.* Go to your local bookstore and head to the magazine section. Look for targeted publications for a certain niche. You're looking for magazines for people who are passionate about something. For example, *Bird Talk* magazine is for people who love birds. *Cat Fancy* magazine is for people who love cats. *Soldier of Fortune* magazine is for people who love guns and related things. *Bass Fishing* magazine is for people who like to fish for bass.

Once you find some of these magazines, look at the ads. See what types of products are being advertised the most. Get a general feel for the market by reading the articles. Constantly ask the question, "What do these people want more than anything?"

If you feel like you're closing in on a market, order some back issues of the magazine and see which ads are being published on a consistent basis. These are the products that are selling and are therefore the products that the market wants.

2. *Clubs and organizations.* Look in your newspaper's classified section for clubs and organizations. Most papers publish a list of local clubs that people can join based on their interest. For example, there are clubs for gardeners, clubs for BMW drivers, clubs for dog lovers, clubs for people who have addictions, clubs for people of various religions, and many more. Browse through these listings and see if anything jumps out at you.

Attend a club meeting and get a feel for what this group is like. Be looking for a universal problem that needs to be solved, a common desire among members, or even a common enemy. Again, ask the question, "What do these people want more than anything?"

■ LOCATING YOUR MARKET ON THE INTERNET

Once you have an idea for a good market, it's time to see if they're easily reached on the Internet. After all, if your market isn't easy to reach, you'll have a hard time getting them to your web site and getting them to buy from you.

Fortunately, you can find out in a matter of minutes. My favorite method is to look at Overture.com. As of this writing, Overture.com has a great little tool called "The Search Term Suggestion Tool." It allows you to type in a word and see how many people searched for it in Overture's network of search engine partners.

For example, let's say you're thinking that parrot owners might be a good market to sell to. You would go to Overture, click on "Advertiser Center," and then click on "Tools" at the top of the page. From the "Tools" menu you would select "Term Suggestion Tool." When the Term Suggestion Tool opens, you would type in "parrots." About two seconds later you would see that 59,467 people searched for the word *parrots* last month. (This number changes every month.)

So now you know that people who love parrots are looking for parrot-related information on the Internet. If only a few hundred people were searching for the word *parrots* every month, then you should change your market. But 59,467 people is a good market.

Now that we've found out that parrot lovers are on the Internet, it's time to find out what they want. One way to do this is by reading their magazines from your local bookstore. Another way is to visit parrot-related web sites and to see what they're about. Subscribe to their e-zines and see what the articles are about.

Yet another way is to find parrot-related newsgroups and read what they're talking about. You can do this by going to Google.com, clicking on "groups," and then doing a search for "parrots." While writing this, I went to Google.com and performed this search. Within seconds I found four newsgroups dedicated to parrots. The first one I clicked on had 158,000 posts. These are posts by people who love parrots. It's like being a fly on the wall at a parrot lovers' convention!

Read the posts and ask yourself the ever-important question: "What do these people want more than anything?" Once you find the answer, you can then start thinking about creating a product and marketing it.

Key Point: There is no sense in guessing what people want. Do your research and find out *exactly* what they want. Then give it to them. It's very easy to sell a person something they already want. How hard is it to convince a kid to eat ice cream? You want the same scenario with your market.

■ THE NEED FOR A NICHE

In order to make real money, you've got to make money while you're sleeping. That means you must find a way to create residual income or, in a business model, sell things when you're not there. Marketing information products through an automated web site is a great way to do that. But how do you choose what products to market? You need to find a niche.

Why is it so important to choose a niche in an online business? The answer is simple: to survive and prosper. It doesn't make economic sense to try to compete with the giants online. Their pockets are a lot deeper than those of the small businessperson or entrepreneur. They can afford staff and expensive advertising. They can reach a wider audience and can hang in there longer if the going gets tough. It's much, much wiser to find a smaller area—a niche—that the big boys are neglecting, and set yourself up as the place to go for that niche.

Most marketers have heard of the 80/20 rule—20 percent of the buyers consume 80 percent of the product volume. If you can identify the 20 percent that allows you to sell more product with much less effort, without much competition, you'll find it easy to succeed.

■ WHAT EXACTLY IS NICHE MARKETING?

You can think of niche marketing as the opposite of mass marketing. Mass marketing attempts to reach the masses. The target market is huge and unspecified—basically, the general population. But niche marketing offers a specialized or focused product or service to a very specific target market.

An online niche is a site that focuses on one thing or one area and does a really good job of it. It provides what the big sites can't or won't. It fills a need or a want for a segment of a larger market in a tightly focused and highly specialized way. Because it's online, it can provide timely, updated information or offer a product or service not available locally.

Niche sites are not as obvious as general sites online. Unless you're in the field and looking for that kind of information, product, or service, you don't know they're there. I think of niche markets as being tucked into a niche in cyberspace. When you step into the niche, a whole universe that revolves around that topic opens up. The beauty of it is, while you can't compete with the giant sites on their level, they can't compete with a good niche site on *any* level.

So take a niche that you know something about. Research its profitability. Find out if there are enough people on the Web interested in that niche. Find out what they want and whether they spend money in that niche. Check out the competition. If all systems are go, then create a site around that niche, offering irresistible products that appeal to your niche clients.

Rufina James and Bart Baggett, owners of http://www.nichemarketingsecrets .com, have recently created "Niche Marketing Secrets," an online e-course explaining how to turn your hobby, special interest, or expertise into a niche market worth over $12,000 a month in your spare time. Their free seven-day preview reveals the secrets and strategies you must know *before you start. Find out more by contacting them at nichesecrets1@proreply.com.*

27

Give Them Reseller Rights

Graham Hamer

Are reseller rights right for you? The answer is yes, they're right for everyone. Let me quickly define *reseller rights* as they apply to Internet marketing.

Scenario one: John writes a great e-book. He sells it for $50. Jane buys it, but she may not sell or give it away. End of chain.

Scenario two: John writes a great e-book. He sells it for $50 with reseller rights. Jane buys it and sells 10 copies for $50 each, also with reseller rights. The 10 people who bought from Jane continue the sales, and so on. The chain has no end.

You might wonder why John would write a great e-book and then allow it to be circulated on the Internet with none of the sales proceeds going back to him. The main reason an author sells rights to his product is to generate leads for other products he sells, or for which he is a reseller. Very rarely, if ever, are you allowed to remove the contact info of a product you bought rights to. So selling another person's product does generate other back-end sales for the product's originator.

With these links in each copy of his e-book, John benefits simply by having his book in circulation. Jane benefits by being able to sell John's book for 100 percent profit. And everybody else in the never-ending chain benefits because they can all do the same thing. Moreover, if John is scrupulous about only recommending products that he has tried, tested, and been totally satisfied with, every reader of his book will benefit from his knowledge and experience. So yes, reseller rights are right for everyone.

In fact, this is viral marketing at its best. And, better still, because John knows that he will get some back-end income from his book, he is prepared to sell it for $50 where normally he would have charged $100. Everyone is a winner.

Are there any drawbacks? Sure there are. Nothing in this world is perfect. As a reseller, you could end up with a product that already has a hot market ready to buy without having to do any of the research, creation, or ad writing. It could be the perfect opportunity. On the other hand, this same "perfect opportunity" might be sold by hundreds of businesses already. It could be outdated. And it may never have sold well in the first place!

Even though I have created my own products, I have still used reprint rights licenses in many ways to either expand or generate new profits. I purchased reprint rights to several products when I first wanted to market online. The early success I experienced through selling these products led to the business I am in today. A quick inventory of my reseller licenses at the moment shows that I have over 30 different e-books that I can give away or sell. (If you're asking why I would give them away, consider all the "extra bonuses" that are offered free on the Web. All of them are products to which the marketer has—or should have—purchased the reseller rights.)

But now I want to come clean with you. The preceding scenario is a somewhat oversimplified version of events. For sure, simple reseller rights do exist. With my own e-book, *TheTrafficJam Formula*, *all* purchasers get the full reseller, redistribution rights. They are free to sell it, give it away, eat it for lunch, read it to the kids at bedtime—anything they want, except alter it. Because I have built in sufficient affiliate links to make it worth my while, I can sell this book at a low price against a vaguely similar (though somewhat outdated) e-book on web site traffic generation, being sold by a so-called traffic guru for $97 with *no* reseller rights. Do you see the difference?

A less simple method of acquiring reseller rights than the one I've outlined is when an e-book sells for $50 without reseller rights or $1,000 with reseller rights! No, that's not a typo. Most reseller rights are sold for between 10 and 25 times the cover price of the book. Often this includes branding, when the author of the e-book will rebrand the affiliate links to those of the reseller. It is understandable, therefore, that the owner should want a premium price for his intellectual property.

Another alternative, which is becoming increasingly popular, is a *shared branding*. That means that most of the internal links will remain unchanged, with the author's codes embedded in them, but the reseller is able to add his or her links to a few primary contacts in the introduction to the book. This is sometimes called *personalizing* the book and is usually available with short reports rather than with longer, in-depth e-books.

Here are a few do's and don'ts to buying reseller rights.

■ DO BUY RESELLER RIGHTS TO GET STARTED ONLINE

I bought low-cost reseller rights for my first couple of years online. They gave me a good foundation. The products were already complete, as were the sales materials that went with them.

Owning a product that you bought rights to can give you a good start. You don't have to worry about writing ads at first or producing a product. You can jump in, get your feet wet, and start learning about online marketing. This first product probably won't make you rich, but it will give you experience for all of your later projects.

■ DO BUY RESELLER RIGHTS TO USE AS BONUS PRODUCTS

Every experienced Internet marketer will tell you that you *must* pile up the bonuses to sell a product. In fact, the bonus items should *outvalue* the actual product you are offering.

Ginsu made this one famous. They were selling a set of steak knives, but before the commercial was finished, you had so many bonus items on the table it was hard to refuse.

Make sure you provide quality bonuses and not some worthless, outdated junk that damages the credibility of your main offer. Quality e-books to which you have the redistribution rights make a perfect bonus.

A word of caution: Make sure you are entitled to give the product away before you do so. Some reseller agreements state a minimum price for which the product must be sold.

■ DO BUY RESELLER RIGHTS FOR BACK-END PRODUCTS

You have your first product out. It is making money, but what about the back end? All direct marketers know that the real profits of business do not come from your first sale to a customer. They come from continually selling over and over to the same customers.

You can expand your product line by purchasing reseller rights to high-quality products. This will help you generate additional cash flow from your prospects and customers.

■ DON'T BUY SOMETHING JUST BECAUSE SOMEONE SAYS IT IS THE BEST OPPORTUNITY EVER

Avoid this type of hype when buying reseller rights. As a beginner, try to find a product you would want to buy yourself. Purchase the retail version first, try it out, and then purchase the rights if you are still interested.

Occasionally, you'll come across a product, like my own *TheTrafficJam Formula*, where buying the retail version automatically gives you the reseller rights. These deals are rare, so well worth exploring.

■ DON'T BUY RESELLER RIGHTS IF YOU DON'T HAVE A MARKET IN MIND

Don't buy a $1,000 reseller rights package if you don't already have a plan in mind to sell it. Just because it is the most awesome book on the planet doesn't mean it will sell. The best situation is when you already have a market lined up to buy from you, such as your own newsletter list or high volumes of daily traffic at your site.

You should examine the product by buying a retail version. Then figure out a way to sell it. *Then* buy the reseller rights. Finally, go for master rights once the reseller rights have started earning you a profit.

■ DON'T BUY RESELLER RIGHTS BY LOOKING THROUGH THE SEARCH ENGINES

Good reseller rights are usually purchased because you are already a customer of the person or company you are buying from. You know they have good products that you can sell.

■ DON'T BUY RESELLER RIGHTS IN A SMALL, SATURATED MARKET

Make sure the product is either pitched in a niche market where demand exceeds supply, or in a mainstream market that would be difficult to saturate.

■ DON'T BUY RESELLER RIGHTS IF THE PRODUCT IS OUTDATED

A lot of people don't offer reseller rights on a product until it is already outdated. Instead of updating it, they sell off the rights to unsuspecting buyers. Make sure the product is fresh.

Reseller rights are right for everyone, though I would add one more word of caution to all budding authors: Make sure you cloak your affiliate links. It is a little-known fact that over 30 percent of all affiliate links are hijacked or chopped by unscrupulous readers! Don't let it happen to you. Invest in an affiliate link cloaker and be safe.

Graham Hamer produces the TopProfits *weekly e-zine of Internet marketing. His e-book* TheTrafficJam Formula—*complete with reseller rights—can be downloaded from TheTrafficJam.com.*

28

Viral Writing: How to Automate Your Writing Like a Virus

Larry Dotson

■ STEP ONE OF THE VIRAL WRITING SYSTEM

One of the easiest and fastest ways to write an e-book is to have others write it for you. You just send one e-mail to a group of knowledgeable people, asking them for related content for the e-book or article you are writing or compiling. I'll give you a sample e-mail or content request. Don't use it as a template. You will have to change it for your own particular information product or article. I would send something like the following e-mail if I wanted to write an e-book with tips about how to increase your e-zine subscribers.

Subject: I need your help?

Dear Friends,

My name is Larry Dotson. If you don't know me I've written a lot of articles and e-books on Internet marketing. You can check out my main web site at http://www.ldpublishing.com.

Like you, I'm always looking for new ways to increase my e-zine subscribers. I'm currently compiling an e-book of tips and ideas on how to increase e-zine subscriptions. These tips will mainly be for e-zine publishers and opt-in mailing list owners. Could you take a few moments to write down some of your best tips and ideas? Please only submit content that you own the intellectual property rights to (e.g., copyrights, trademarks, patents, etc.).

I will be selling the e-book. Though I can't offer you payment for your content, I can give you a free copy of the e-book once it's finished. It will be a win-win situation for all of us. I'll get free content and you'll get an e-book full of new tips and ideas. Also, feel free to plug your web site or business underneath your tips. Just imagine, if this e-book is a best-seller, everyone who buys this e-book will see your ad and possibly buy your product.

After I receive your replies, I'll compile them into one e-book. I may or may not use all of your tips. If I need to edit any of the tips, I'll contact you to get your final approval and permission. Please e-mail your tips and ideas to bizreport@sssnet.com or visit my web site to use the automated form: http://www.ldpublishing.com. Please let me know of any questions and concerns you might have.

Sincerely,

Larry Dotson

P.S. I will need the tips submitted by Aug. 23, 2002, or I won't be able to use them. Also, you'll lose out on the free copy of the e-book and a plug for your business.

■ STEP TWO OF THE VIRAL WRITING SYSTEM

At the end of the content request, I would also say something like this: "If you don't know any good ideas, please forward this message to someone you know who does," or "Please forward this message to someone you know who might be interested in contributing," or "If you know anyone else who might like to contribute, please forward them my offer." Your message will spread to other people who will give you content for your information product. And then those people might send it to people they know, and so on. Just like a virus!

■ STEP THREE OF THE VIRAL WRITING SYSTEM

Once your information product or article is nearly ready or complete, you can add something like this at the beginning or end of it: "If you have any good tips or ideas for increasing e-zine subscribers which weren't included in this e-book and you want to donate them to me at (e-mail address), I may use them to create an e-book or article on this same subject. Rest assured, I will get your final approval if I decide to do so. And I will give you a free copy of the e-book or article once it's complete. If you know anyone else who might like to contribute, please tell them about my offer."

Here's another approach: "If you know of any other strategies for increasing e-zine subscribers, please e-mail them to me at (e-mail address). If I get enough, I might write a follow-up or sequel to this e-book. I will get your final approval if I decide to do so. And I will allow you to put an ad for your business at the end of the e-book. If you know anyone else who might like to contribute, please tell them about my offer."

By adding that statement you may get enough content to create back-end and up-sell products. If you only receive a few submissions, you could use them to write a promotional article for the information product you're selling. This can also help you create updates for your information product. The ideas are endless.

Bonus idea: You could also ask people for content about other topics if you know what your next information product or article will be about.

Do you now see how easy and profitable viral writing can be? Now let's look at some detailed pointers to make viral wiring work for you.

■ SEVEN WAYS TO WRITE AN INFO PRODUCT BY SENDING ONE E-MAIL

1. Specific information products: If you want specific tips, strategies, ideas, processes, and so forth, you could begin your query with something like "I'm currently compiling an e-book of romantic date ideas."

2. General information products: If you want a wide range of tips and ideas to which you could always add on, your approach could be, "I'm currently compiling an e-book of tips and ideas about all aspects of e-zine publishing and promotions—for example, content ideas, strategies for increasing subscribers, the e-zine creation process, and so on."

3. Interview/real-life information products: If you want to interview or profile experts about a subject, just use a list of predetermined questions. You could say, "I'm currently compiling an e-book that will include interviews from 20 of the top online marketers. If you would like to be one of them, just answer this list of questions . . ."

4. Short-story information products: If you want a collection of fiction or nonfiction short stories (or just one), like success stories, children's stories, case studies, fiction stories, and so on, your query could begin, "I'm currently compiling an e-book that will contain five short stories on how people decided to start their own business. If you want to share your story or experience . . ."

5. Free article information products: If you're looking for already published articles, information, or excerpts on a general or specific topic, your request could start, "I'm currently compiling an e-book of articles relating to online marketing. If you would like to include your article . . ."

6. Directory information products: If you want a list of resources like e-zines, web sites, web rings, off-line locations, experts, and so forth, you could say, "I'm currently compiling a directory of e-zines that swap e-zine ads, which will be in e-book format. If you want your e-zine listed, just fill out the information below . . ."

7. Collection information products: If you want a collection of things like sales letters, recipes, reviews, poems, templates, graphics, and so forth, you could say, "I'm currently compiling a collection of classified ads that people can use as templates or ideas for creating their own ads. If you want to donate any of your ads, just . . ."

■ 16 IMPORTANT ELEMENTS TO INCLUDE IN YOUR CONTENT REQUESTS

You can use all or some of these elements in your requests.

1. Make sure the group of people you are sending your content request to are educated in the information or subject you are seeking. If they are not, it will be a waste of time. For example, if your own e-zine is about online marketing, it would not be a good idea to send a content request for gardening tips.

2. Make sure you set a time frame or a deadline by which you need or want the content. This will get people to act faster and help you get your project completed faster or on time.

3. Make sure to personalize your message, if possible. It will grab people's attention and they will read your request for content quicker. It also won't look like you're sending it to hundreds of thousands of people. If you can't personalize it, it would be a good idea to use one of the following phrases in your subject box or headline: "I need your help!" "Can you help me?" "Can you do me a favor?" Most people have been taught that they should help people in need or that it's only polite to do a small favor for someone. Another option would be to use the benefit you're offering them, like "A Free E-Book!" "Get Free Publicity!" and so on.

4. Make sure you introduce yourself and/or your business. Give any helpful or persuasive background information, like telling them what you both have in common; it will help them like you and give up their content quicker. Also tell them anything that will show your authority or credibility so they will feel trust in giving their content to you.

5. Use vivid descriptions of what they will get in return for giving you their content. Make it appeal to their senses and imagination. Also, use any metaphors, stories, and analogies that would be persuasive.

6. Make sure your content request looks and sounds professional. You don't want to have spelling or grammatical mistakes. Always proofread it several times. Keep it organized and logical. Make the request sound simple. Highlight any important or persuasive words and phrases. Write it the way you talk. Make sure a child could understand it. Use short words, sentences, and paragraphs. Use positive words. It should be clear and easy to read. It should be free of jargon they wouldn't understand.

7. Give your audience a compliment or two. Flattery does work. Include information that leads them to believe you know them personally. Most people think they're smart, right? You could say, "I just had to ask you first because I know how educated and experienced you are in increasing your own e-zine subscribers."

8. Be sure to sound human. Show your emotions. If you're excited and enthused about your information product offer, they will be, too, and will be glad to give you some content. Use exclamation points and smiley faces, and capitalize emotional words.

9. Make sure you give people a few choices or options. It'll make them feel like it's their own idea to submit their content to you. For example, "I allow you to either get the e-book for free and place your ad at the end of the e-book, or get a discount on the e-book and plug your ad at the beginning of the e-book."

10. Include words like *win/win, benefit, profit, gain, fair, equal,* and so on. This will help persuade them that you both win.

11. Make them feel like they are getting more out of the deal. Offer them a huge list of incentives—for example, free things to give away, cash, discounts, free advertising, percentage of sales, and so on. You could also put the dollar amount beside each item or total it up at the end. This will show them what a bargain they are getting.

12. Clearly explain how you will be using the contributor's content in your information product. If they don't understand, they may not give it to you. Plus you don't want any misunderstandings that could cause problems down the road for you. Here are some details you may need to explain:

➤ Are you going to be selling it?

➤ Are you going to be giving it away?

➤ Are you going to allow others to give it away?

➤ Are you going to be selling the reprint rights?

➤ Are you going to be offering an affiliate program?

➤ Are you going to be selling the master reprint rights?

➤ Are you going to be selling the customization rights?

➤ Are you going to be converting it to other info formats?

13. Make sure you are specific about the content you are seeking. You don't want a bunch of content that you don't need. This will also save you time—you won't have to resend your e-mail request.

14. Make sure you are protected. It would be a good idea to have your lawyer write up a clause that protects you from being liable from content that these people submit to your e-book or information product. For instance, the person may not be the rightful copyright, trademark, or patent owner of the content. The content could be damaging in some way to people reading it. Use any other clause or disclaimer your lawyer recommends. You could include it in both your e-mail request and your information product.

15. Make sure to get contributors' final approval if you have to edit or change their content submissions in any way. If you don't want to edit or proofread, or don't know how to, you could offer an editor or proofreader a plug in your e-book in exchange for their services.

16. Make sure your content request contains all the information they need to make a formal decision, but leave room for negotiation, questions, or concerns. For example, you might end with, "Please let me know any questions and concerns you might have." Also, be prepared to answer any questions that the people might have.

■ 10 PLACES TO SEND YOUR CONTENT REQUESTS

You will likely only need to use one of these methods, depending on how populated they are. If you want your e-book to be huge, you may want to send your one e-mail to multiple places.

1. Send it to your list of e-zine subscribers.
2. Send it to a related e-mail discussion list that will allow it.
3. Send the e-mail and bcc (blind carbon copy) to a targeted group of knowledgeable people or experts that you have selected.
4. Post it into a related chat room that will allow it.
5. Post the e-mail on a related message board that will allow it.
6. Post the e-mail on a related web blog that will allow it.
7. Trade or buy a space in another e-zine to send your e-mail message.
8. Post your e-mail on your web site.
9. Set the request up as an automated form on your web site and lead people there from your e-mail.
10. Trade or buy a space on another web site to post your e-mail.

■ 12 WAYS TO PERSUADE PEOPLE TO GIVE UP THEIR CONTENT OR IDEAS

1. Offer them a free plug for their business, product, web site, and so forth.
2. Offer them a free copy of the information product once it's done.
3. Offer them a discount on the information product when it's done.
4. Offer them a discount on another product you sell.
5. Offer them a free product that you normally sell.

6. Offer them the first opportunity to join your affiliate program.

7. Offer them the reprint rights or master reprint rights to the information product.

8. Offer them a free ad on your web site or in your e-zine.

9. Offer them an e-book, a free copy of the information product with their own customized affiliate links (if you allow people to give it away as a viral marketing tool).

10. Offer them a free membership (if you are starting an information product membership site).

11. Offer them a free copy of the information along with free monthly or yearly updates to it.

12. Offer them up-front money, like $5 per tip or in the form of a contest. You could say, "You'll win $100 if your idea is chosen to be published on the first page!"

■ A REAL LIFE EXAMPLE OF VIRAL WRITING

My friend Joe Vitale sent me and others the following content request e-mail. Though he didn't use all the viral steps I talked about earlier, it still worked!

Subject: I need your help

Date: Sat, 2 Mar 2002 10:54:59 -0600

From: "Joe Vitale" <jgvitale@ix.netcom.com>

To: "joe Vitale" <me@mrfire.com>

I'm speaking in New Orleans on March 14 on "Outrageous Marketing for Free Newspapers."

I'm collecting ideas to help these publishers better market themselves. They primarily need to build their subscriber base and bring in more advertisers. Would you take a few minutes and jot down some ideas on how they can do that? This would greatly help me, as well as them. I might collect the replies I get, put them in a report, and hand them out, which would give you a little free publicity. So feel free to plug a book or web site of yours, if you like. I want this to be a win-win-win for all. If you want a little more information about these free newspaper publishers and their challenges, see the article below, sent to me by a key figure in the association.

I am very grateful for any help you can give me, and them.

Thank you,

Joe

P.S. Since I speak in less than two weeks, time is important.

> One of the constant themes that comes up at conferences could be "We (our papers) don't get no respect"—from advertising agencies, and from major regional accounts in our markets. Small and medium size advertisers who advertise in our member papers get great results and continue to advertise, but in many markets we can't land the large accounts we would like. These ads often go to the daily papers, even though they often have a smaller distribution and higher rates. Some papers are very strong with auto dealers; some have a great grocery following; and many are strong with private party classified, but we don't do as well with regional accounts.

> The huge box stores that are coming to markets all across America are a threat to free papers. Our strength has been with the small and medium size businesses who are closing and going to work for Wal-Mart, Home Depot, etc.

Chapter 29 is the information product Joe created with this one e-mail.

Larry Dotson is the prolific author of numerous e-books, including many written with Joe Vitale. His main site is at www.ldpublishing.com.

29

Outrageous Marketing
for Free Newspapers

Joe Vitale

I don't know it all. No one person does. So I went to my peers and asked for their help. What follows is a priceless collection of amazing, wild, surprising, fun, easy, zany, and sometimes even sexy ideas from marketing specialists and others, compiled for a publishers marketing conference held March 14, 2002, in New Orleans. I e-mailed about 15 marketing specialists, told them of the conference and the needs of the participants, and invited them to brainstorm ideas for this topic. Here are their replies. These aren't edited, but they're all potential gems. Which one will do the trick for you? Beats me. But let me know!

■ FROM JAY CONRAD LEVINSON

(Jay is king of the guerrilla marketers, reachable at: www.jayconrad levinson.com. His latest book is *Guerrilla Creativity*.)

About 40 years ago, when I was working for an ad agency in Chicago, we prepared a pro bono ad for newspapers. The theme was "What if there were no newspapers?" Lots of ad agencies entered the contest, and several of the ads were run in the *Tribune* and *Sun-Times*. I think having such a contest will draw attention to newspapers and underscore the importance of advertising in them and subscribing to them.

I also think advertisers should be aware that regardless of the growth of the Internet, the newspaper remains the best medium for local companies to count on for heavy lifting.

A good idea would be to make a list of about 25 advertisers who have used free newspapers for 10 years or more. They certainly wouldn't continue to advertise there if they weren't getting superb results. It doesn't matter if nobody has heard of the advertisers; the point is that they have learned for themselves the joy of *Pennysavers* and such.

Remember, the people who go to huge box stores still read newspapers; still look for bargains; still want to avoid the cold, impersonal atmosphere of the Home Depots of the world; and still wish to connect with their communities. I think it's the sense of community that has made AOL so successful, and I believe that free newspapers feed into this need for community. Even the huge box stores will take on even more of a local flavor if they advertise in local free newspapers.

Finally, smart newspapers will give a copy of *Guerrilla Marketing*, Third Edition, to potential advertisers. And they'll send cogent postcards to potential subscribers.

Good luck in Louisiana, y'all!

■ FROM MIKE DOOLEY

(Mike, the author of *Infinite Possibilities*, is reachable at www.tut .com/auwc.htm.)

What if there was only *you* . . . and the rest of the world was make-believe, imagination? if even the people in your life were drawn there, or faded away, based upon *your* thoughts? Would it then be easier for you to grasp the true meaning of *limitless*? Would you then believe that *you alone* make your reality? My friend, the rest of the world *is* make-believe, imagination—and all the people in your life *are* there, or fade away, based upon *your* thoughts. Have a Play-doh kind of day. Tallyho!

■ FROM LARRY DOTSON

(Larry is coauthor of *The Hypnotic Writer's Swipe File*, available at http://www.hypnoticwritingswipefile.com.)

Here are 15 ideas that I threw together quickly.

1. Work for long-term advertising income. Give advertisers two or three advertisements for free if they agree to buy six more ads in the next year or two. (Record/CD companies use this principle.)

2. Offer advertisers a free online ad with every ad they buy. Create an e-book version of their newspaper and give it away free (like viral marketing). This will increase subscriptions as well as advertising income.

3. Allow one big-name company (like Wal-Mart) to advertise for free if they give you a testimonial. The rest of the big-name companies should follow.

4. Increase your subscriber base by making something in your newspaper collectible or relating it to a current, popular fad or news story.

5. Hire a writer to embed or interweave the ads into the content of the newspapers. He or she could also write short advertorials for each individual advertiser. The advertisers should get a higher response than in the big-name newspapers.

6. Increase your subscriber base and advertisers by giving businesses discounts to advertisers in exchange for them displaying or advertising your free newspaper in their place of business or online.

7. Give advertisers a discount when they spend more than a certain dollar amount for ad space. You can also apply this tip to the number of ads they buy.

8. Offer advertisers a free bonus for renewing their ad order. It could be an e-book, special report, online utility, and so forth.

9. Sell advertising space between your content. You just break your content in half and insert the ad between.

10. Guarantee your customers advertising results. If they don't like the response they receive, give them a refund or another ad for free.

11. Offer to endorse the product your customers are advertising before or after their ad runs. In all honesty, you would have to try out the product first. Endorsements usually pull higher than traditional ads.

12. Write a review for your customer's product to place under their ad. This is similar to a testimonial or endorsement but more in-depth.

13. Make your advertising revenue by creating a wholesale ad membership. Advertisers could pay so much a year to get discounted ads in your newspaper. Even if they don't take advantage of the discounts, you still make money.

14. Sell a subscription or per-issue ad-free version of your newspaper and forget about ad revenue. People will pay not to see ads in their publications because they see ads everywhere and get tired of them—on TV, on billboards, on the Internet, almost everywhere they look.

15. Create joint ventures with other similar publishers, so that when one of you sells an ad, you split the revenue and the ad runs in all the publications. You all work together.

■ FROM SHEL HOROWITZ

(Shel is the author of *Grassroots Marketing: Getting Noticed in a Noisy World*, available at http://www.frugalmarketing.com.)

I think in places where there no longer exists a local daily, free papers have an opportunity to brand themselves as the hometown newspaper. This requires actually reporting on the city council, the school board, the high school football team, a police log, and so on. Word will spread very quickly once they make the shift. Then, of course, they can capitalize on the additional readers in terms of ad base.

■ FROM BOB BLY

(A copywriter and consultant, Bob can be reached at http://www.bly.com or http://www.surefirecustomerservicetechniques.com.)

The industry should prepare a white paper (or hire Joe Vitale to do it) that says, "Yes, small papers in some way do *not* deserve re-spect journalistically. We are a service to the community, not Wood-ward and Bernstein. Our reporting is more service oriented than investigative. Where we *should* get your respect is in our CPM re-sults: We cost *less* to reach your target prospects"—do calculations to demonstrate this—"yet ads in small papers actually do *better* than larger dailies in terms of response." You can research this or at least show it anecdotally. "So if you want a Pulitzer, we are the wrong place to go; if you want customers, we are the best and most afford-able place to go."

■ FROM KARE ANDERSON

(Author, speaker, and trainer, Kare is reachable at www.sayitbetter.com.)

Perhaps cross-promotion would help them get advertisers and readers. Their sales staff might suggest to current and prospective ad-vertisers that they make joint promotions in their ads to leverage more visibility and value out of their advertising budget. Perhaps the sales people can offer a "Ten ways to attract more customers with less mar-keting dollars" tip sheet (also send as a PDF).

Make it easy for advertisers to display their ads on-site by provid-ing them with a museum-quality (thick, not thin) Plexiglas stand im-printed with these words: "As seen in (name of free newspaper)." Provide copies of the advertisement tear sheet in the front of the stand and copies of the current issue behind the tear sheet, for customers to take. This would attract new readers.

■ FROM BLAIR WARREN

(Blair is a persuasion expert, TV producer, and author of the book *The Forbidden Keys to Persuasion*. He's at www.BlairWarren.com.)

Here are two ways to counteract the "don't get no respect" problem:

1. Team up with medium that already does get respect: talk ra-dio. Arrange a barter/trade-off relationship with a local radio station to promote your paper in exchange for ink promoting their station. Perhaps offer a DJ or two the opportunity to have their own column in the paper, furthering their exposure and increasing their popularity in their market. If the DJ can't write, offer to ghostwrite the column. It could be something as simple as an editorial or a movie review. The point is to give them exposure in order to give you exposure.

You could also have a few major advertisers mentioned every time your paper is mentioned on the radio. For example, an announcer could say, "Brought to you by ABC Newspaper and XYZ Autoplex"; the next time it would be "by ABC Newspaper and Appliance World." This cross-media promotion would sweeten the pot for the newspaper's bigger advertisers (i.e., they get newspaper space *and* radio airtime with one purchase). Being on the radio will help build respect for, awareness of, and interest in a paper.

2. Collect "I love you" quotes from readers and advertisers, and use them in two ways. First, pepper them throughout each and every issue of your paper to convey a sense of reader/advertiser loyalty. And second, bundle them together and use them to pitch potential advertisers. List several of them, then say something like: "Only one newspaper has earned this much respect from its readers and advertisers. No, not (insert competitor's pay newspaper here). It's (insert free newspaper's name here). That's right. Our local *free* paper. When it comes to local loyalty and effectiveness, nothing can deliver like we can."

■ FROM BOB BURG

(Bob is the author of *Endless Referrals* and *Winning without Intimidation*, and the publisher of the *Winning without Intimidation* e-zine, at www.burg.com.)

One thing that comes to mind is that, when a prospect doesn't see or believe that the seller can provide the benefit they claim, then a steady dose of proof might be what they need. Of course, testimonial letters are always great for this. I might suggest attacking this both from a local and national point.

For example, can these individual local owners network with their national counterparts and begin doing an exchange of testimonials for every industry they wish to sell on the local level? This way they can show that not only does it work here, but (and especially if they have no proof *yet* of it working here) it's been proven in all of these other markets to work with a similar business such as the prospect's.

Now, the objection they may get is that, "Sure, it will work in Tuscaloosa, or Bridgeport, or Dallas, but it won't work here in my town." For that, the seller will have to develop a response that brings up similarities or other convincing factors.

■ FROM GREG MANNING

(Greg publishes *The Seaside Sun*, a free visitors and entertainment guide, in Corpus Christi, Texas.)

Here are eight quick thoughts regarding free newspapers:

1. Be professional, and fulfill commitments and deadlines. Respect is hard to earn but easy to lose. (We are fighting the reputation of the previous owner of our paper.)

2. Follow Joe's rule: ask how you can best serve the advertiser— and *listen*. Too often we are too busy selling to hear what the customer needs.

3. Invest in one or two local trade shows a year. There are businesses who want to advertise but may be unaware that you even exist! (Another Corpus Christi free newspaper increased their ad revenue 35 percent after attending a local trade show.)

4. Obtain sponsors for specific columns. One lawyer sponsors a crossword puzzle, while a record store sponsors a listing of the local radio station programs. It is also easier to sell a long-term advertising contract this way.

5. Increase desirability by allowing exclusivity when possible. Since 80 percent of our papers go to visitors, we have an "Emergency Care" section that lists a doctor, a dentist, a chiropractor, a veterinarian, and a pharmacy for each of five local towns. Note: Other health professionals are welcome to advertise in other areas of the paper; they just don't get the instant recognition that this section provides.

6. Correlate an article featuring a specific business, event, or other news piece with an appropriate advertisement. For example, a recent article featured the benefits of a certain dietary supplement. We sold an ad to a local health food and nutrition center that advertised its brand of that supplement.

7. Barter for promotion of the newspaper. Exchange airtime with local radio stations for printed advertisement. Everyone wins.

8. If the paper is placed in specific businesses for distribution, enlist their financial support. Emphasize the value to their customers and the service you are giving to their business. If the business owner does realize the value your paper is contributing to his or her business, ask for an ad each quarter or so.

■ FROM PAUL J. KRUPIN

(Paul is the author of *How to Make the Media Fall in Love with You* and *Trash Proof News Releases*. He also operates IMEDIAFAX.com, the Internet to Media Fax Service, a custom news release distribution service.)

I spoke in Los Angeles to the Book Publicists of Southern California one year on Valentine's Day. It was a delightful, catered affair, with drinks, dinner, and dessert. I gave my talk to a packed room of about 130 people at the Sportsman's Lounge in Studio City. I explained "How to Make the Media Fall in Love with You" by telling story after story, demonstrating and analyzing media responses to news releases for books, innovative products, and other news events.

The bottom-line results show amazing similarity in media expectations. If I had the penultimate maximum editor or producer right here in front of me, and I asked her, "What would you want from me if I could get a feature article?" she'd likely say, "Tell me a story (a short, bedtime story), give me a local news angle (of interest to my particular audience), hit me in the pocketbook (make me or save me money), teach me something I didn't know before (educate me), amaze me or astound me (make me say *wow!*), make my stomach churn (in horror or fear), or turn me on (yes, sex sizzles)."

So what you have to do to get media coverage is give the media what they want! And guess what—what they really want turns out to be what most people in America want. Surprise! Look around you and you'll see that all news coverage is basically designed to cater to what the American public wants the most.

And if you look around you, you'll see that this is really easy to identify. It's everywhere. It's simple to see. And once you see it, a light will go on. I've boiled it all down to one simple formula: DPAA+H. These letters stand for "Dramatic Personal Achievement in the face of Adversity, plus a little Humor." If you look at almost all the media around you, from the front page of *USA Today* to the Olympics to the evening news to the sitcoms on TV, you'll see this is what the American public wants, desires, even craves.

As a culture, we crave to see the human spirit triumph in matters of the heart and in trials of life, love, beauty, hardship, and tragedy. We ask to be uplifted right out of the humdrum of our everyday reality into the exhilaration of extreme emotions and sensations experienced up front, close, and personal by those living life on the absolute cutting edge of human experience.

We are addicted to the spice of life. It galvanizes our attention. It rivets us to our seats. It captures our hearts. We look for it in what we read, what we watch, and what we listen to. We ask to be placed right into the shoes of those in the spotlight. And this is what the media seek to provide. This is what works. This is what keeps the public glued to their seats.

You will see these elements everywhere you look, in varying degrees. It is a rare media feature that doesn't contain these items. The media use technology to increase the intensity of our experience, assault our senses, enhance the effect, entrance us, intoxicate us, and make our experience ever more compelling and memorable. If you are seeking media coverage, you have to recognize this insane desire and need, and then cater to it.

Do your best to write a news release so that it interests as many people in the audience as possible. Ask yourself who these people are and talk to them. Do your homework and know who your book, product, or service will appeal to. Then write your news release so that it tells a story.

Describe the five W's quickly—the what, who, where, when, and why—in dramatic personal adversity and achievement terms. This helps you cast your spell to the widest possible audience. Make it snap, crackle, and pop, and make it easy for the media executive to get it right away.

There's a real business reason why this works. Media are publishers, and you need to look at them as publishers—in business, trying to do what all of us are trying to do: make a living. Good news readily converts to more subscriptions or market share for advertising dollars. So when you write a news release, say this to your media prospect: "Fellow publisher, will you give me space in your publication?" or "Fellow publisher, will you give me airtime on your show?" Then put yourself in his shoes, and understand that the media executive is going to ask the following question: "Is this better than everything else I have today?" The answer determines his bottom line—revenue!

So grab today's newspaper, and start thinking about it with a new set of eyes. Use DPAA+H. If there are more dramatic personal stories of achievement in the face of adversity, plus a little humor, available that day, you lose. If not, you win. But one thing is certain: If you learn how to use DPAA+H you will get more media coverage.

> *I believe in advertising all the time. There is no such thing as getting a business so established that it does not need to advertise. Babies who never heard about you are being born every day, and people who once knew you forget you if you don't keep them reminded constantly. Dull times are the very times when you need advertising most.*
>
> —William Wrigley Jr. (1861–1932), who made a fortune selling something few had heard of in his time: gum

■ FROM BOB EASTER

(Bob published a newspaper for some 25 years and is now an author of books on buying and selling homes. He established in two months a free 200,000-copy publication delivered to every household in Palm Beach County on a weekly basis, while at the same time marketing the daily/Sunday newspapers, plus another daily and five other weekly publications. Find out more at www.easterhome.com.)

Think outside the box to increase your net income. Take your eye off the target and you miss your market. Here are nine ways to stay on target.

1. Rethink your position. The number one issue with daily publications is that subscription coverage is declining and advertising rates are climbing. These two weaknesses can be a gold mine if you use them correctly. Have a rate card with a chart showing the cost per thousand readers (never call them subscribers) and another chart that shows the low percentage of subscribers in the neighborhood. (Use the Audit Bureau of Circulations—ABC—against them.)

2. Just for now, acknowledge that you might never land the big accounts because of the media buying habits of major corporations. Start making a list of small stores you are not reaching now, using the following guidelines to attract future business.

➤ Make a wish list of the types of stores you want to attract to your publication. If you need to upgrade the type of advertising in your newspaper, then set goals to replace ads that lower your image with readers. There are all kinds of small businesses that your publication can successfully help.

➤ Design a series of types of ads that you know will pull customers into a business. Give the advertisers a choice of using any one of the five different types which have a proven way of attracting new customers, then walk in and give them an offer they can't refuse—a free ad to try your publication. Make sure the ad has an already proven coupon in the copy. In other words, set up only proven successful ads and make a believer out of your new customer.

Note: For the publisher who is counting the cost of a free ad, ask another question: "What is it costing me not to offer a different approach and not to have the new account advertising with me?"

➤ Establish a buddy system where advertisers who are currently steady customers would receive a coupon discount good for color in their ad or dollars off a new ad in the future, when they bring in a new advertiser who is on your priority list.

Businesspeople know other businesspeople, and you need them to talk up your publication. It's like getting a new sales force without having to hire and pay new people. The added benefit is that their friend is now talking about your publication.

➤ If you are building coverage in a small area around a neighborhood shopping center, deliver free samples to each home within a mile radius during a blitz campaign. Make sure you have an ad in your publication that shows readers where your publication is distributed free each week. Also, ask each store in the shopping center to hand the publication out to shoppers. For each store that agrees, give a nice prize at a local eating establishment, such as a coupon good for one entree when another is purchased—and give the owner of the restaurant a free ad in exchange for coupons.

Note: A home delivery blitz should last at least four weeks, and your plastic bag cover should read "Free Coupons Inside."

3. Acknowledge that not all small businesses are potential advertisers. Go after the target accounts only.

4. Ask readers by means of a survey what they enjoy or like about your product. Also, go after garage sales, resale shops, local hardware stores, and so on.

5. Look at the way you distribute free copies. Exactly how clean are your news racks? Remember, the appearance of a newsstand or rack states to the public how you regard your product. You can move 25 percent more copies on a rack with a clean appearance. (This has been proven by a major daily newspaper.)

6. Your front page conveys the image you want to project, and it is where the reader makes a determination to read or not read. Come up with a new, colorful design that makes a reader want to pick it up week after week.

7. Look at deadlines. Are they proven ones that help sell advertising, or do they hinder advertisers? Who determined the publication day, and how long ago?

8. Who publishes the most successful free newspapers and why? Start making a list of the successful ones and list the top five reasons. Then compare the list against your practices. Where can you improve?

9. Sell sections crammed full of helpful home tips, remodeling information, and household budget stretchers, which the consumer will keep and use.

■ BONUS SECTION

And here are 34 more ideas.

1. Adopt a stretch of road in your state's litter clean-up program.
2. Create a personality. (Think Betty Crocker, Mickey Mouse, Pillsbury Doughboy.)
3. Create a weekly mystery. Describe someone in your community with an unusual hobby but don't say who it is. Ask, "Who is Mr. X?" Reveal it next week.
4. Add crossword puzzles. Give the answers in the next issue.
5. Offer a chance to win a vacation package. It's free to the winning reader. Give a free ad to the travel agency that offers the package.
6. Get a controversial columnist to write weekly fiery articles.
7. Publish poems by children.
8. Hold a beauty contest, a baby contest, or an animal contest.
9. Give free e-books to readers.
10. Conduct a poll or survey on a weekly basis. Give results in the next issue.
11. Create a sandwich board campaign. Get people to wear the boards to advertise your publication.
12. Start an association—it can be humorous or real.
13. Run for political office.
14. Model *Reader's Digest*: Have first-person stories, humor, a new word of the week, and so on.
15. Throw a party—or crash a party.

16. Create a comic strip.

17. Read the book *There's a Customer Born Every Minute*, by Joe Vitale. Do a forced-creativity exercise with it, or with any book. Open it anywhere and make what you find there solve a problem or give you an insight.

18. Listen to "The Power of Outrageous Marketing," by Joe Vitale. (See www.nightingale.com.)

19. Model *Maui Weekly*, published by Joe Sugarman. (See it at http://www.mauiweekly.com.)

20. Ask for help. Network. Reach out. Connect with other businesses that serve the same people you do. Create win-win-win cross-promotions with them.

21. Educate yourself. For example, you can start my free e-mail marketing course, "Easy Marketing Secrets," by sending a blank e-mail to hypnoticmarketing@getresponse.com.

22. Create satisfaction-conviction guarantees for your advertisers. Say, "Advertise in my paper 10 times. I guarantee you will get results. If you don't, I'll give you a free round-trip ticket to Vegas."

23. Teach advertisers how to advertise. Hold a seminar at lunch time, offer free food, and teach them the three proven ad types: open letter, advertorial, and direct response.

24. Always remember that people in your community are interested in people in your community. Find the unusual, the human interest, the unique. Remember that people are interested in themselves first and other people second. Three surefire attention grabbers are women, babies, and pets.

25. Send postcards to potential advertisers, announcing your satisfaction-conviction guarantee (see number 22), or some other offer.

26. Ask yourself, "What would P.T. Barnum do?" Expand your mind. Have fun!

27. Write a book or booklet. This gives you added credibility and an excuse for publicity. It can lead to fame, fortune, and immortality.

28. Remember that "Intention rules the earth" (Oprah). Set intentions for your day, your meetings, your newspaper. Do the five steps in *The Attractor Factor*.

29. Visualize and *feel* the results you want, as if already done. Be the end result. Read "Being the Solution" at http://hop .clickbank.net/?outrageous/being.

30. Invite readers to write in with questions, suggestions, letters to editors, recipes, jokes, first-person stories. It's the *Chicken Soup for the Soul* approach. They write, you publish.

31. Announce that one issue each week will have a real $100 check in it. All the other issues will have fake checks embedded in ads. Advertisers will fight to get the ad space, knowing that readers will look closely at each check, hoping it's the real one.

32. Visit my web site for dozens of free marketing articles. It's at http://www.mrfire.com.

33. Invite advertisers to place inserts, not just ads, in paper.

34. Get Joe Sugarman's books: *Advertising Secrets of the Written Word, Marketing Secrets of a Mail Order Maverick, Television Secrets for Marketing Success,* and *Triggers.*

30

Thirty-Nine Ways to Create an E-Book with Little or No Writing

Joe Vitale

Use the strategies you learned in Chapter 28 ("Viral Writing") to apply these ideas.

1. *Ask for specific pieces of information.* Send an e-mail to a group of people, asking them for one specific piece of information, such as tips for writing classified ads.

2. *Ask for general pieces of information.* In an e-mail to a group of people, ask for a more general piece of information, such as online marketing strategies. This can elicit a wider range of responses than the more specific request in the previous tip.

3. *Do multiple interviews.* E-mail a group of people, asking them to answer a short list of specific questions. For example, provide a list of questions about themselves and their business, skills, expertise, career, hobbies, and so on.

4. *Do one full interview.* Send an e-mail to one person, asking him or her to answer a huge list of predetermined questions. You should create enough questions to fill up a short e-book (e.g., 5 to 20 pages) after the person answers them. It would almost be a biography.

5. *Record a long, one-on-one conversation.* Invite one person to have a conversation with you about a specific topic. You could do this by phone, recording it and then getting it transcribed into text for your e-book. Or you could have the conversation via e-mail, chat room, message board, or instant message, and then copy and paste it into e-book format.

6. *Record multiple short conversations.* Contact several people, requesting that each of them converse with you about a specific topic. Again, the resulting e-book could consist of transcribed telephone conversations, or you could have the conversations via e-mail, chat rooms, message boards, or instant messages, and then copy and paste them all into e-book format.

7. *Record a group conversation.* Invite a small group of people to join in a group conversation with you about a specific topic. You can record it over the phone (via a teleconference line) and get it transcribed into text for your e-book; or have the conversation via e-mail discussion list, chat room, or message board, and then copy and paste it into e-book format. Another possibility is to get everyone together in person at a suitable location—for example, at your home, office, lunch setting, or conference room—and record, then transcribe, the conversation.

8. *Hold a seminar.* Invite a small group of people to speak at your seminar about a related subject. Then record the whole seminar and transcribe suitable portions for your e-book. You could also hold the seminar over the phone (teleseminar) or via chat room, audio conferencing, or video conferencing.

9. *Request original articles.* Ask several writers to each write a short, original article about a specific subject. Of course, you could offer them incentives to do this. Compile all the articles into e-book format.

10. *Ask for recommended resources.* Send an e-mail to a group of people, asking them to recommend a resource for a specific type of project. For example, what web sites do they recommend for submitting free e-books? This will reduce the amount of research you have to do. Then ask the web sites' owners for permission to list their web sites in your e-book, and invite them to write their own descriptions for their web site listings. Your e-book would be a collection of links with descriptions to lead people to these resources.

11. *Compile recommended information resources.* Send an e-mail to a group of people asking them to recommend a resource for a specific subject or type of information, such as web sites that publish free viral marketing information. Again, ask the owners for permission to list sites in your e-book and invite them to write their own descriptions of their web sites.

12. *Link to the information or resources you want.* Find the places you want to link to, using search engines, online directories, and other online references. Get the permission of the webmasters, authors, publishers, or owners, and invite them to write a short description for their link. Your e-book will be full of links with descriptions, to lead people to the references or information you find helpful.

13. *Get excerpts from message boards, forums, newsgroups, and e-mail discussion lists.* Send an e-mail to community participants, asking permission to use either an excerpt of a posting or the full posting on a certain topic.

14. *Get excerpts from web site content and articles.* Send an e-mail to web site owners, asking them for excerpts from their content or articles on a specific topic for your e-book.

15. *Get excerpts from e-zines.* Ask e-zine publishers for permission to use specific excerpts from their e-zine for your e-book.

16. *Get excerpts from online or off-line videos or audios.* Seek permission from the creators of video or audio materials to use specific excerpts for your e-book. You would have to transcribe the excerpts, unless the owners already have transcriptions available.

17. *Get excerpts from e-books.* Send an e-mail to authors or publishers, asking permission to use specific excerpts from their e-books for your own e-book.

18. *Get excerpts from membership sites.* Request permission to use specific excerpts from membership web sites in creating your e-book.

19. *Get excerpts from e-reports.* Send an e-mail to the author or publisher of an e-report, asking permission to use either an excerpt or the full e-report in your e-book.

20. *Get excerpts from e-courses.* Ask authors for permission to use an excerpt from their e-course, or the full e-course, in your e-book.

21. *Get excerpts from off-line subscription publications.* Contact authors and publishers to request permission to use excerpts from their articles, essays, reports, or other content previously published in newspapers, newsletters, magazines, and the like.

22. *Get excerpts from books.* Contact authors and publishers and ask their permission to use excerpts from their books for your e-book.

23. *Compile a collection.* Send an e-mail to a group of people asking them for a collection of things you could compile together into an e-book. For example, you could put a collection of recipes into an e-book that people could use as a reference. Other ideas would be poems, product reviews, photos, short stories, and so on.

24. *Do multiple human profiles.* Ask people to fill out a form with topics about their personal life and preferences. For example, you could ask them where they were born, their favorite color, their hobbies, and so forth. Compile these profiles into an e-book.

25. *Do multiple nonhuman profiles.* Ask a group of people to fill out a profile about things they own or know about. For example, you could ask webmasters to profile their web sites and include categories like number of pages, average visitors, freebies they offer, and so on.

26. *Create templates or tools.* Send an e-mail to a group of people, asking them for a collection of content that could be used as tools, templates, or models for others. For example, you could ask for sample sales letters that other people could use as templates or models to write their own sales letter. Other ideas include business letters, drawings, classified ads, headlines, or romantic letters.

27. *Take multiple online surveys or polls.* Ask a group of people to fill out a long survey or poll, and compile the answers into an e-book. The questions can be fill-in-the-blank or multiple-choice format. For example, if your e-book is about gardening, you can ask things like how often they water their garden, what fertilizers they use, and how they get rid of weeds. This is almost like an interview but you provide choices.

28. *Rewrite someone else's information.* Send an e-mail to authors and publishers, asking their permission to add to, rewrite, or update a piece of their information to use in your e-book.

29. *Rewrite or add to someone else's information product.* Send an e-mail to one author or publisher, asking permission to add to, rewrite, retitle, update, subtract from, and/or change the format of their information product so you can turn it into an e-book for yourself. You could also rewrite it in a way to sell it to a more specific or different target audience—for example, rewrite a general how-to marketing e-book so it is specific to the accounting profession.

30. *Coauthor an e-book.* Invite writers or experts to coauthor an e-book with you. You could have one or more coauthors. The more coauthors you have, the less you'll have to write. You may end up writing only the title and table of contents. Offer the coauthors free publicity.

31. *Compile archived information.* Ask authors and publishers if you could create an e-book using their archived information, such as old e-zine issues, articles, reports, free reprint articles, stories, and so on.

32. *Create a directory.* Announce to a group of people that you are creating a directory in e-book format, and ask them if they want to contribute. For example, you could tell them you're creating an e-book directory of resources that accept paid advertising. These could include e-zines, web sites, message boards, software freebies, businesses, and off-line resources. Use a pre-made form that enables them to fill out their information, like other online directories do.

33. *Ask for unpublished manuscripts.* Contact known writers and publishers and ask them if they have any unpublished manuscripts about a certain topic. Offer to sell these for them in e-book format if you can be listed as the coauthor or copublisher. This could be as simple as copying and pasting your name and business in place as the coauthor or copublisher. You would reward them with a percentage of sales or free publicity.

34. *Ask to convert other information products.* Ask known writers and publishers if they would like to have their information product converted into e-book format. Again, offer to sell it for them in e-book format if you can be listed as the coauthor or copublisher. You can give them a percentage of sales and/or free publicity.

35. *Buy the reprint or master reprint rights.* Buy the reprint or master reprint rights to someone else's e-book for 100 percent profit. You could use tips 1 through 34 to create your own e-book bonus for the product (if the original owners allow you to).

36. *Join an affiliate program.* Join an affiliate program to sell someone else's e-book for commission. Again, use tips 1 through 34 to create your own e-book bonus for the affiliate product, if the owners agree.

37. *Find an e-book with no affiliate program.* Find an e-book being sold with no affiliate program and offer to sell it for the author in exchange for a percentage of the sales. You could create an affiliate program where you're the sole affiliate to get your commission. Use the previous tips to create your own e-book bonus for the e-book if the author agrees.

38. *Trade reprint rights.* Use tips 1 through 34 above to create your own e-book, then trade the reprint rights for the reprint rights for another e-book.

39. *Compile for reprint rights.* Compile other people's information into e-books for them in exchange for the reprint rights to the e-book.

31

E-Book Selling Tools

Larry Dotson

■ FORTY-SEVEN TIPS FOR SELLING E-BOOKS

Tell your potential customers some key facts and figures about your e-book. I begin with five here, along with some helpful ad copy phrases.

1. The number of helpful links and resources.
2. How long it took you to write or compile your e-book.
   ➤ "(Number) years in the making . . ."
   ➤ "It took (number) hours to create this . . ."
   ➤ "Spent countless hours researching . . ."
3. The number of pages in your e-book.
   ➤ "(Number) information-packed pages . . ."
   ➤ "Countless pages of . . ."
4. The number of chapters or lessons.
   ➤ "(Number) information-rich chapters . . ."
   ➤ "(Number) knowledge-packed lessons . . ."
5. How big the e-book's download file is.
   ➤ "(Number) KB of information."
   ➤ "Over (number) MB of information."

A Tip from Joe Sugarman

My quick tip for anyone wanting to make money online fast is twofold:

First, read my book *Triggers*. It contains 30 ways to persuade people to buy from you, online or off. More importantly, there is one method in there so powerful—I am using it right now—it will almost force you to go buy my book right now. (Yes, you'll have to get my book and read about this powerful concept on page 163 to understand what I'm doing here.)

Second, sell my book *Triggers*, as well as all my other books, at your web site. This is not just an attempt to get more people to sell my books. This is a sincere way for you to have an instant product and to make money selling it right now. To get details on my books, go to www.JosephSugarman.com and click the "Earn Money Fast" button.

There you have it: two ways to make money online fast. Will you act on them? Most won't. The few who do will prosper, online or off.

(Joe Sugarman is the author of several books and is considered a legend in the direct mail and infomercial business. His main web site is www.blueblocker.com.)

Include information about the originality of your e-book and any fringe benefits available to the buyer, such as reprint rights and affiliate programs. Again, here are some possible scenarios with helpful ad phrases you can use.

6. The originality of the information in your e-book.
   ➤ "100 percent original information."
   ➤ "No filler information."
   ➤ "No rehashed information."

7. Reprint or master reprint rights.
   ➤ "100 percent royalty-free resell rights."
   ➤ "Keep 100 percent of each sale."

- ➤ "Free reprint rights."
- ➤ "Free resell rights."
- ➤ "Royalty-free reprint rights."
- ➤ "Sell an unlimited number of copies."
- ➤ "Sell as many copies as you want."

8. An affiliate program in which only a few sales will pay for the purchase.
   - ➤ "(Number) affiliate sales will pay for it."
   - ➤ "Sell (number) and make back your money."

9. Full-time customer service and help available with purchase of your e-book.
   - ➤ "24 hours a day, 7 days a week."
   - ➤ "24/7 customer service."
   - ➤ "Call anytime toll-free."

10. Ability to sell the e-book and earn commissions.
    - ➤ "Comes with free reseller program."
    - ➤ "Join our affiliate program."
    - ➤ "Earn money selling this e-book."

Customers want to be assured of the validity and accessibility of the information in your e-book. Use the phrases offered here to increase their confidence in your product.

11. Tell your potential customers your e-book is a complete resource on the subject.
    - ➤ "Covers every detail."
    - ➤ "Covers everything."
    - ➤ "All in one place."
    - ➤ "It's all covered in . . ."
    - ➤ "It's all here."

12. Let them know it's available in other formats.
    - ➤ "Available in hard copy format."
    - ➤ "Listen to the audio version."

13. Tell them it's based on real-life experience.

➤ "Based on a true story."

➤ "Based on my life experiences."

➤ "Real-world examples."

14. Assure potential customers that your e-book will answer all their questions.

➤ "Answers hundreds of your questions."

➤ "It won't leave your questions unanswered."

15. Let them know your e-book is popular.

➤ "Best-seller."

➤ "Best-selling."

➤ "Over (number) copies sold in (number) days!"

➤ "People from all over the world have bought it."

16. Let people know your e-book can be accessed in minutes or seconds after ordering.

➤ "Can be instantly downloaded."

➤ "Download it in minutes."

➤ "Fast and easy access."

➤ "Immediately downloadable."

17. Tell them your e-book is easy to understand.

➤ "Clear language."

➤ "Clearly explained."

➤ "Clearly written."

➤ "Easy to understand."

➤ "Easy to read."

➤ "Written so a baby could understand it."

➤ "Written in everyday language."

➤ "Written in plain English."

➤ "Jargon free."

➤ "Straightforward."

➤ "Straight-to-the-point information."

18. State that your e-book is easy to follow.
   - ➤ "Step-by-step instructions."
   - ➤ "Takes you step-by-step . . ."
   - ➤ "Highly organized."
   - ➤ "Simple to follow outline."
   - ➤ "It walks you through . . ."
   - ➤ "Helps you every step of the way."

Convince your customers that purchasing your e-book is not only a special opportunity but something they will continue to value for a long time to come.

19. Tell your potential customers they can only buy your e-book at your web site.
   - ➤ "You won't find this in (location)."
   - ➤ "You won't see this anywhere else."

20. Promise to send regularly scheduled, free updates of your e-book.
   - ➤ "Up-to-the-minute updates."
   - ➤ "Updated weekly."
   - ➤ "Free monthly updates."

21. Tell your potential customers they will learn secret information inside your e-book.
   - ➤ "Unlike any other."
   - ➤ "Uncover insider techniques."
   - ➤ "Uncommon information."
   - ➤ "Never before seen information."
   - ➤ "Never-heard-of information."
   - ➤ "Learn closely guarded . . ."
   - ➤ "Experts won't share this."
   - ➤ "Behind-the-scenes look . . ."

22. Assure them that you don't hold any information back.
    ➤ "Uncensored."
    ➤ "Everything exposed."
    ➤ "Everything from . . . to . . ."
    ➤ "Spill my guts."
    ➤ "Learning everything from A to Z."
    ➤ "Learn everything from start to finish."

23. Tell them how much time they'll save by buying your e-book.
    ➤ "Save yourself years of research."
    ➤ "We've researched everything for you."
    ➤ "Don't waste your time researching."

24. Show them why buying your e-book would be a great bargain, by breaking down the expense into concrete terms.
    ➤ "Only spending ($) per day."
    ➤ "Only spending ($) per tip."
    ➤ "Only investing ($) per benefit."
    ➤ "Only investing ($) per chapter."
    ➤ "Only paying ($) per page."
    ➤ "Only paying ($) per word."

25. Tell your potential customers that your e-book has the newest information.
    ➤ "No outdated information."
    ➤ "No recycled information."
    ➤ "No rehashed information."
    ➤ "No same-old information."
    ➤ "A fresh approach."
    ➤ "A new twist."
    ➤ "Discover new tricks."
    ➤ "Exclusive information."
    ➤ "Fresh information."
    ➤ "Latest information."

26. Let them know that your e-book is easy to use and navigate through.
    - ➤ "Fully searchable."
    - ➤ "Clickable chapters and pages."
    - ➤ "Highly organized."
    - ➤ "Easy navigation."
    - ➤ "Organized table of contents."
    - ➤ "Over (number) searchable chapters."
    - ➤ "User-friendly."

27. Tell them who endorses your e-book.
    - ➤ "Endorsed by . . ."
    - ➤ "Readers say . . ."
    - ➤ "Here's what others are saying."
    - ➤ "Comments from some satisfied customers."
    - ➤ "Here are some testimonials."
    - ➤ "See what experts say."

28. Assure your potential customers that they don't have to be an expert to learn your information.
    - ➤ "For a beginner or pro."
    - ➤ "For a novice or expert."
    - ➤ "Great for beginners."

29. Offer them the chance to read a sample excerpt or chapter from your e-book.
    - ➤ "Free trial download."
    - ➤ "Take a look at the table of contents."
    - ➤ "Download a free version of . . ."
    - ➤ "Get a sneak peak at some . . ."
    - ➤ "Free excerpt."

30. Tell your potential customers your e-book is packed with information.
    - ➤ "Endless supply of information."
    - ➤ "Advice-jammed."

➤ "A wealth of information."
➤ "A huge collection of . . ."
➤ "A massive collection of . . ."
➤ "A gold mine of information."
➤ "A full archive of . . ."
➤ "Crammed full of . . ."
➤ "Chock full of . . ."
➤ "Jam-packed."

31. Assure them that your e-book is accurate.
    ➤ "Accurate information."
    ➤ "Cold hard facts."
    ➤ "Thoroughly researched."
    ➤ "No misinformation."

32. Tell your potential customers they can customize the e-book with their own links.
    ➤ "Add your own links."
    ➤ "Customize this e-book."

33. Tell them your e-book is a valuable reference that they will use again and again.
    ➤ "Encyclopedia-like."
    ➤ "Easy reference."
    ➤ "Handy reference."
    ➤ "A deluxe reference."
    ➤ "Essential reference."
    ➤ "Helpful reference."
    ➤ "Right at your fingertips."
    ➤ "Think of it as your personal companion."

34. Tell your potential customers that the information is proven.
    ➤ "Time-tested."
    ➤ "Proven strategies."

➤ "Battle tested."

➤ "100 percent tested and proven."

35. State that you're only selling a limited number of copies.

➤ "Order before they are gone."

➤ "Limited edition e-book."

➤ "Order before (day, date, time)."

➤ "Copies are limited."

36. Promise that there's no risk at all in ordering your e-book.

➤ "Risk-free."

➤ "Guaranteed."

➤ "I personally guarantee . . ."

➤ "Double your money back."

➤ "All the risk is on me."

37. Offer free bonuses.

➤ "Free consulting."

➤ "Free report."

➤ "Get (number) bonuses!"

➤ "(Number) free gifts!"

➤ "You'll get ($) worth of bonus gifts!"

➤ "Get (number) freebies valued at ($)."

38. Tell your potential customers your e-book includes classic information.

➤ "A (year) classic."

➤ "Forgotten secrets."

➤ "Ancient secrets."

➤ "Classic."

➤ "Timeless information."

➤ "Timely ideas."

➤ "Rare strategies."

39. Tell your potential customers your e-book is collectible.

➤ "Limited edition."

➤ "Only selling (number) of this version."

➤ "Add it to your series."

➤ "Only (number) autographed copies left."

40. Show them how your information will pay for their purchase price.

➤ "Just one (benefit) will pay for it."

➤ "This tip alone is worth . . ."

41. State when your e-book will be or was released.

➤ "Just published."

➤ "Just released."

➤ "Will be released (date)."

➤ "Reserve your copy."

42. Demonstrate your credibility as an author or expert.

➤ "I have a (type of) degree in (subject)."

➤ "I've taught (number) seminars about . . ."

➤ "I've written over (number) (books, articles, etc.) on . . ."

43. Tell your potential customers how detailed your e-book is.

➤ "Detailed description of . . ."

➤ "Detailed report."

➤ "Detailed table of contents."

➤ "Exactly how to . . ."

➤ "In depth."

➤ "In-depth report."

➤ "Specific instructions."

➤ "Precise details."

44. Describe all the benefits of your e-book using a bulleted list under a given topic.

➤ "How to . . ."

➤ "Discover which . . ."

➤ "(Number) hot reasons . . ."

➤ "A blueprint for . . ."

➤ "Learn how to . . ."

➤ "The hidden secrets . . ."

45. Emphasize repeated or new selling points using a P.S. or strong closing.

➤ "Remember, all the bonuses . . ."

➤ "As stated earlier . . ."

➤ "Remember you have the option of . . ."

➤ "If you're not totally convinced yet . . ."

46. Offer plenty of ways to order.

➤ "Secure online ordering."

➤ "Bill me later."

➤ "We accept online checks."

➤ "Pay by major credit card."

47. Grab customers' attention with a good headline.

➤ "How to . . ."

➤ "Discover . . ."

➤ "Imagine . . ."

➤ "Attention . . ."

➤ "Warning . . ."

■ HOW TO SUCCESSFULLY SELL INFORMATION PRODUCTS THAT ARE UNEDITED

If you don't want to worry about grammar, spelling, punctuation, and the like, you could market your information product as research, as an unedited/uncut version, or as notes. For example, "My lost and forgotten notes on Internet marketing—buy them now, unedited and uncut!"

You could also warn your readers at the beginning of your information product that you realize there may be errors in it, and give them a reason. Joe Vitale did this in his "Outrageous Marketing for Free Newspapers" (see Chapter 29). Another idea is to tell your prospects you are holding a contest. For example, "Whoever finds the most grammar, spelling, and punctuation mistakes in my new e-book will win $100!" That alone might give people an incentive to purchase your e-book.

■ SIXTY-TWO IDEAS FOR A BUSINESS-RELATED E-BOOK THAT OTHERS CAN WRITE FOR YOU

Using the strategies you learned in Chapter 28 on viral writing, send an e-mail to a group of people asking them for tips about one specific piece of information. Here is a list of possible topics to get you started.

1. Increasing e-zine subscribers.
2. Starting a free e-zine.
3. Writing free reprint articles.
4. Writing classified ads.
5. Writing a sales letter.
6. Creating an e-book.
7. Selling an e-book.
8. Picking an affiliate program to join.
9. Ranking high in search engines.
10. Selling an affiliate product for commission.
11. Promoting a free e-book.
12. Creating a membership web site.

Jim Donovan on E-Zines

Something that's worked well for me as a writer is to offer my articles for free to people who publish e-zines in my subject areas. Many of the larger e-zine publishers are not writers or have such a heavy publication schedule that they are thrilled to accept articles that fit their readership. These then lead interested people back to my site where they can buy my books and learn more about me.

I also offer affiliate programs so people can earn extra income by helping me promote my products. If, for example, a person has an e-zine that reaches independent business owners, publicizing and offering links to my book *Marketing Your Own Business* can earn them extra income *and* help their readers. Win-win-win!

If I were starting out, I'd build a list of local business events in my area (something nearly impossible to find) and offer it as an e-zine. I'd then sell advertising in it to those businesses who want to reach the small business owner. There are a lot of big global sites but little being done on a local scale. A woman I know used to do such an e-zine and it was the most valuable resource around. By covering all the available small business events, networking groups, meetings, and so on, you give people a one-stop resource that exceeds what any single newspaper is capable of covering.

(Jim Donovan is the author of *Marketing Your Own Business* and *Handbook to a Happier Life*. His web site is www.jimdonovan.com.)

---

13. Taking credit cards.

14. Increasing web site traffic.

15. Creating an e-course.

16. Promoting an e-course.

17. Selling back-end products.

18. Following up with customers.

19. Up-selling products.
20. Creating mini sites.
21. Creating joint venture deals.
22. Writing endorsements.
23. Using viral marketing.
24. Getting free advertising.
25. Bartering goods and services.
26. Selling reprint rights.
27. Buying reprint rights.
28. Designing a web site.
29. Writing business proposals.
30. Creating a contest.
31. Promoting a contest.
32. Starting an affiliate program.
33. Promoting an affiliate program.
34. Starting an online business.
35. Running an online business.
36. Selling advertising space.
37. Writing information products.
38. Promoting information products.
39. Selling at online auctions.
40. Reducing costs and expenses.
41. Negotiating with other businesses.
42. Building an opt-in list.
43. Beating the competition.
44. Creating a niche.
45. Staying organized.
46. Picking a product to promote.
47. Starting an online community.
48. Promoting an online community.
49. Getting free publicity.

50. Using online customer service.
51. Writing press releases.
52. Using online persuasion.
53. Creating banner ads.
54. Creating pop-up ads.
55. Brainstorming new product ideas.
56. Improving products.
57. Increasing target markets.
58. Finding products to resell.
59. Increasing inbound links.
60. Pricing products.
61. Increasing e-zine readership.
62. Increasing web site readership.

32

Magnetic Internet Power Marketing

Frank Kern

The reason so many web sites fail is simply this: People have been fed a lot of misinformation about successful Internet marketing. Right now, everywhere you look you'll hear the same thing—so-called "gurus" telling you that all you have to do is get a bunch of hits to your site and you'll make more money than you ever thought possible. It's pretty easy to buy into this theory, isn't it?

When I first started marketing online, I had the same inner conversation with myself most Internet newbies have when they get started. The conversation sounded something like this:

"Well, let's see here. . . . If I can get 10,000 hits to my web site, that will be pretty good. And let's say that, worst-case scenario, only one half of one percent of them order. Okay, so one half of one percent of 10,000 is 50 sales! Wow! If my product brings me $97 per sale and I get 50 sales then I'll make $4,850.00! So if I can just get 10,000 hits every couple of weeks, I'll be rich! And you know what? My product is so darn good that I bet I'll get more than one half of one percent of my visitors to buy it. I bet I'll get 10 percent or more. This is going to be so easy!"

Have you ever talked to yourself like this, poised over the calculator with dollar signs in your eyes? Well, if you believe the biggest lie about Internet marketing, then this conversation makes perfect sense. But I say the "hits equals sales" theory is not true. Here's why.

Hardly anyone *ever* buys anything the first time they visit a web site. In fact, studies have determined that it takes a typical Internet customer an average of *seven* visits to a web site before they buy anything—and that's assuming that you have a good offer, good credibility, and good sales copy on your web site. With that fact in mind, you can see why simply getting a lot of hits on your web site is not the answer. If you're just depending on hits, you're in trouble. Sure, you might get a few sales from hits alone, but you'll have to work like a maniac to keep enough traffic coming in to amount to anything. And the few orders that come your way most likely won't make you enough money to be worth the hassle.

This is why so many web sites fail. The owners spend a small fortune to drive traffic to their sites but the sales don't come like they expected. So they walk away muttering that the Internet "just doesn't work" or "it's all just a bunch of hype." It's true—a lot of information out there is just hype. In fact, most of the information about Internet marketing is recycled drivel that was effective a few years ago but doesn't work now.

So what can you do? You have to think outside of the box. In this case, we're going to think outside of the Internet entirely and steal an incredibly powerful marketing strategy from a totally different industry: mail order.

■ HOW YOU CAN USE A "STOLEN" SECRET FROM A DIFFERENT INDUSTRY TO DRIVE YOUR INTERNET INCOME THROUGH THE ROOF

My definition of marketing is setting up automatic, repeatable systems that create the environment where people want to buy from you—instead of you having to sell them.

—Jeff Paul

It's really much easier to make money on the Internet if you know the right formula and use the right tools. In fact, once you get everything in place, you can pretty much run your business by remote control.

When I first tried to make money on the Internet, I went about it all wrong. I wasted tons of money on advertising and worked like a slave to drive hits to my web site. I was trying to sell people on my products, instead of creating an environment where they wanted to buy from me. Sure, I got some traffic, but I didn't get orders.

Then I stumbled across a how-to book from a totally different industry that opened my eyes once and for all. It showed me how to really make money on the Web without having to be a salesman! It was a book about how to make money in mail order, by a direct marketing genius named Jeff Paul. The title was *How to Make $4,000 a Day from Your Kitchen Table Sitting in Your Underwear.* I still smile when I read that title, but the great thing is that Jeff Paul actually did make $4,000 per day while sitting at home in his underwear! The book basically said that he made a tremendous fortune in mail order by adding a simple little twist to his marketing.

Here's what he did: Instead of mailing his sales letter to a big list of people who had never heard of him (the mail order equivalent of just getting a lot of hits to your web site), he ran tiny, dirt-cheap ads that offered a free report about what he was selling. All the people had to do to get the free report was to give him their name and address, and he would mail it right out to them. Once he received their name and address, he would send them his sales letter along with some very useful information.

And here's where it gets good: Jeff stayed in touch with his prospects. He would continue to send them sales letters along with valuable information in a predetermined sequence, until they bought from him!

What Jeff did was create a relationship with his prospects. Because he gave them valuable information along with his sales letters, he created an environment where people wanted to buy from him. They never viewed him as a salesman but instead saw him as a trusted adviser.

This sounds like it's too easy to work well, doesn't it? But here's how well it worked for Jeff Paul: Just by using this simple method, Jeff went from living in his sister's basement to making $4,000 per *day* from home in his own little mail order business. It took less than a few months to achieve this once he started using this method.

What does this have to do with Internet marketing? I asked myself the same question. After all, Jeff was in mail order. That's a totally different venue. But once I figured out how to apply this techinque to the Internet, my income soared. And it seemed to happen almost overnight. In fact, my simple homemade web site that sold books and tapes brought in $115,476.21 in the first 12 months!

■ HOW DOES THIS APPLY TO THE INTERNET?

The Internet is just like mail order . . . but without the mail.
—Dan Kennedy and Michael Kimble,
$8,000-per-day direct marketing consultants

First of all, the Internet is just like mail order—but without the mail. Think about it: Isn't a well-made web site nothing more than a sales letter? And when you get a lot of hits to your web site, isn't it the same as sending out sales letters to people in the mail? Of course it is! The basic marketing principles for the Internet are the same as mail order. The only major difference is the speed with which you can deliver information to your prospects—and the speed at which they can buy from you.

Let's take what mail order millionaire Jeff Paul did and apply it to the Internet. Instead of working like crazy just to get a lot of people to visit your web site (and read your sales letter), what would happen if you got people to request free information from you via e-mail? It would be like having a big crowd of people raise their hands and say, "Hey! We're interested in buying from you! Please send us your sales material!" If these interested people read your sales material, do you think you'll get any orders? Of course you will! You know they're interested in your product because they specifically asked you for information!

Remember our earlier discussion about how it takes the average Internet customer a minimum of seven visits to a web site before they buy anything? If you get people to request information from you about your product (instead of sending them straight to your web site, where they'll most likely leave without buying anyway), you will get more sales—guaranteed!

Here's why this will work better than anything you've ever tried, hands down.

Because these people gave you their e-mail address and said, "Hey, I'm interested in what you have . . . please send me some info about it," they have given you permission to send them sales materials and updates as often as you want until they buy from you or ask you to stop. And if you send them good information along with your sales materials, they will grow to respect you as an expert in your field and look forward to hearing from you! You already know it takes most people at least seven times before they will buy anything online. So the more you follow up with your prospects, the more they will visit your site, order your products, and refer you to others. You can then make even more money by sending your prospects offers for other products, such as affiliate programs.

The bottom line is this: Instead of just getting hits, you want people to give you their permission to send them information via e-mail. Once you have this permission, you begin to establish a relationship with your prospects that is beneficial to them, and built on trust. It's what Robert Allen, author of the *New York Times* best-selling book *Multiple Streams of Internet Income* (Wiley), refers to as "going deep."

> Going deep means that you position yourself as the in-depth expert on what your [prospects] want . . . and you create a deepening relationship with them. A lifetime relationship. As the relationship deepens, they will buy from you more products, services, and information at increasingly higher prices—because price will not be the issue.

The reason for this is that they trust you. Because you've given them free information of value and positioned yourself as an expert, they no longer see you as just another person out there saying, "Gimme your money." They see you as a friend and adviser.

But we still have one very important question to answer, perhaps the most important question of all: "How do I get people to come to my site and request the information in the first place?" This is where Magnetic Internet Power Marketing really comes into play. The answer is that you will make more money by giving things away.

■ GET MORE ORDERS JUST BY GIVING THINGS AWAY

Which one of these two options do you think more people will respond to:

1. Visit my web site and buy something! Click here: www .blahblahblah.com.
2. Get a free report: "How to Double Your Internet Income in 90 Days or Less." Click here for instant e-mail delivery.

Of course the second one will get the most response. After all, it's far easier to give something away than it is to sell something, right? And people are going to be much more receptive to your offer if you've given them something of value before you try to make the sale. You go from being just another salesperson to being a trusted friend and adviser. It's just common sense!

And that's what Magnetic Internet Power Marketing is all about: using lead-generation magnets to generate a constant stream of interested, targeted, and qualified visitors to your web site, who then give you their permission to repeatedly contact them with your information.

Here's exactly how this works:

Instead of promoting your web site (which is the same as saying "Hey, come give me money!"), advertise a lead-generation magnet instead. A lead-generation magnet is usually a free piece of information (like a free report) that is valuable to your customers. And it is always related to your product or service.

For example, let's say you were selling the Super Tomato Peeler 2000. Instead of advertising your web site, you would advertise a lead-generation magnet, like one of these examples:

➤ Free report: Top 10 Ways to Peel More Tomatoes.
➤ Free report: How to Peel 8.23 Tomatoes in Less Time than It Takes You to Peel One Tomato Now.
➤ Free e-book: Insider Secrets to Hassle-Free Tomato Peeling.

When people request your lead-generation magnet, they do so by e-mail. They either fill out a form on your web site or send a blank message to an autoresponder. We'll cover exactly how to set this up in just a few minutes, but let's stick with the details of your lead-generation magnet for now.

This next part is very important: Your lead-generation magnet *must* contain valuable information for it to be effective. In other words, your free report needs to be more than just a sales letter for your product. You have to give your prospects something of value for this to really work well. In this example, you give them great information about peeling tomatoes. You tell them of the latest techniques for faster tomato peeling, the best place to find great-tasting tomatoes, and so forth.

But at the end of your report, you tell how the Super Tomato Peeler 2000 can deliver all of the great new things that you just mentioned. You then list a few benefits and put a link to your web site.

If you oversell, you'll lose credibility. Remember, you don't want to come across as being just another person out there looking for a buck. You want to be the tomato peeling expert and a valued friend to tomato peeling enthusiasts world wide. If you position yourself as an expert source of valued information, you will get more sales and you'll get more referrals. Be a consultant to your prospects—not a salesman.

Think about it another way. How do you view your doctor? Most likely you see him as a valued provider of important information. He's your medical consultant, and if he says to go to the store and buy a certain medicine, you'll most likely do it. Similarly, your customers need to perceive you as a trusted consultant. And they will, if you use lead-generation magnets instead of over-used pushy sales techniques. Just remember that if you give something of value before you ask for money, you'll get more sales.

Now it's time for you to meet the king.

■ ALL HAIL THE KING

When you're using Magnetic Internet Power Marketing to promote lead-generation magnets, you not only become a trusted adviser to your prospects and experience an increase in sales, you also develop your greatest (and most overlooked) asset: your own personal opt-in e-mail list.

In fact, the world's top marketing gurus, from Jay Abraham to Marlon Sanders to Jonathan Mizel to Mike Enlow to Dan Kennedy, will all agree on this one statement: *The list is king.* A good, well bonded opt-in e-mail list is like money in the bank for you. If you use it correctly, it's like having the ability to legally print as much cash as you want.

Here's why. When you acquire prospects' e-mail addresses by offering them a lead-generation magnet, you immediately get on their good side because you've just given them something of value for free. As you build a solid relationship built on trust with your customers and prospects, you are lowering their level of sales resistance. The more they become familiar with you, the less skeptical they become and the more they will buy from you. And, if you treat your opt-in list well, they will not only buy from you but they'll also buy from people that you recommend!

In fact, many successful entreprenuers on the Web don't even have their own products. They just use lead-generation magnets to build a large opt-in list, and then they promote affiliate programs to their list.

So here's what you want to accomplish with Magnetic Internet Power Marketing:

➤ Use lead-generation magnets in your advertising to pull in significantly higher response than traditional "give me money" ads.

➤ Lower sales resistance by giving valuable information to your prospects before asking for money.

➤ Build credibility by standing out from the crowd and becoming a valued provider of information.

➤ Steadily (and often very quickly) create your own personal opt-in e-mail list that you can repeatedly make offers to.

Okay, now it's time to give you step-by-step instructions for tying all of this info together and putting Magnetic Internet Power Marketing to work for you.

■ GETTING A MAGNETIC INTERNET POWER MARKETING SYSTEM IN PLACE IN 24 HOURS OR LESS

Let's go over the mechanical details of how Magnetic Internet Power Marketing works. Please note—and this is very important: in order for this to work well, you absolutely *must* have a good follow-up autoresponder system in place. I tell you how to get one in this section, but first let's review the steps.

Step 1: Instead of advertising your web site in the usual "give me money" fashion, use a lead-generation magnet. A sample ad would be: "Free Report Reveals 17 New Ways To Peel Tomatoes! Click Here For Instant Delivery."

Step 2: When prospects click on the link in your ad, one of these two things must automatically happen:

1. They get taken to a page on your web site where they fill in their name and e-mail address to request the free report. When they submit the information in your form, they automatically get fed into your follow-up autoresponder system.
2. They automatically get prompted to send a blank e-mail to your autoresponder system.

Step 3: Your autoresponder system instantly sends them their free report. Remember, you need to provide them with good information as well as a link back to your web site and a reason for buying your product.

Step 4: Your autoresponder system automatically sends them follow-up information at pre-set time intervals that you determine. The system remembers their name and other personal data that you tell it to, so each follow-up message looks like you sat down and wrote it personally. And each follow-up letter contains a reason to buy your product, coupled with useful information.

Step 5: Some of your prospects will buy from you as soon as they get their free report. However, studies show that the vast majority of Internet buyers only purchase after they visit a web site seven times. So, as your autoresponder sends out your follow-up information, you'll notice that your sales increase over time.

When you attract a prospect with a lead-generation magnet, you accomplish the following:

➤ Drive more traffic to begin with by offering valuable information for free, and therefore increase your up-front sales—people who order the first time they visit your site.

➤ Reap the benefits of follow-up sales as you continue to communicate with your prospects.

➤ Build an extremely valuable list of prospects who trust and respect you as an expert in your field.

➤ Make additional profits as you roll out more offers to your list. (These can be products that you create or affiliate programs that you promote.)

And here's another great thing about Magnetic Internet Power Marketing: Once you set up your marketing system, your business is run on autopilot!

The only real work you do is in Step 1 when you place an ad for your lead-generation magnet. Your web site and autoresponder system do the rest of the work for you.

Autoresponders (also called smart bots, mail bots, smart responders, and more) have been around the Internet for quite a while, and people rave about how much they increase sales and make life easier. One source for autoresponders is Hotresponders.com.

Let's say someone responds to one of your ads or goes to your web site and requests free information from you about your product (a lead-generation magnet). As soon as your prospect requests your information, your autoresponder instantly sends them your sales material! It will then remember their name, e-mail address, and any other important information that you want it to. It can also automatically personalize your message so it looks like you sat down at the computer and personally wrote it out just for that particular prospect. You can also preprogram follow-up messages that will be automatically sent to your prospects at predetermined time intervals. The more you follow up with your prospects, the more likely they are to buy from you—again and again.

Frank Kern is the co-creator of the Underachiever System. He has pioneered many "unorthodox" Internet marketing techniques and his niche marketing methods have helped thousands of people achieve financial freedom.

33

The Surgeon's Curve

Christian H. Godefroy

■ BUILDING TRUST AND GETTING PAID

Many people fear being manipulated or misled on the Internet. Many don't like to give their credit card number—it's so easy to steal.

I have found that when I offer to let people pay *after* receiving the goods, I get five times more orders. Why? I can think of three good reasons:

1. They can check that my product is worth what they pay for.
2. They don't have to make a big decision now, so it's easier to order.
3. Since I trust them, they trust me.

Everybody knows that the mail order business has exploded when the "free trial" was invented. It can do much better for you. You see, when someone does not pay you, the only problem is *when* he will pay. If you send him follow-ups, he will pay one day or another. But the mail order business has a big problem: the cost of these follow-ups. They have to stop sending letters someday because the postage costs too much. On the Internet this cost is zero.

Here is my secret mechanism: When someone orders one of my CDs on http://www.positive-club.com, his order goes to an autoresponder (www.aweber.com). The autoresponder replies and confirms the order. If during the ensuing 21 days my customer pays, I remove him from the autoresponder. If he does not pay, he will receive a follow-up 40 days later. Another reminder will be sent 21 days later, and another and another, every 21 days until he pays. After one yet 87 percent of my customers have paid their bill.

What about the remaining 13 percent? Even if they don't pay, since I am selling information, the cost is so low compared to the price that I can allow myself to lose that—especially since my profit has been 400 percent higher than with up-front payment.

Are you wondering why 21 days? That's what we call "the surgeon's curve." When a patient has an operation, if the surgeon sends him a bill before 21 days, he is perceived as greedy. If he waits more, the bill is not paid: The patient forgets that the guy saved his life. Twenty-one days is the best time span: The surgeon is still a hero, and it's good timing to get the money.

When I started to sell on the Internet, I was expecting 2 percent of sales—and got them. With this approach, I get 10 percent or more! One out of 10 of my freebie seekers buys my product! If you sell shoes or cars on the Internet, I don't say that my approach is the best for you. But if you sell information, try it. Compare. Count. You might have a wonderful surprise—and never ask for money up front anymore.

Christian H. Godefroy is the author of How to Write Letters That Sell *and the webmaster of http://www.positive-club.com.*

34

Launching a Successful E-Mail Campaign

Peggy McColl

When I launched my first online campaign for my first book, *On Being . . . The Creator of Your Destiny*, I had no previous experience. Yet the end result was over $30,000 in product sales! No previous experience is required to launch an online campaign. If you follow a few simple guidelines of the experts, like Joe Vitale, you will meet with success.

Here are seven key steps that will help you achieve great success with your first e-mail campaign:

1. Find people (the experts) who have already achieved the results that you want. Ask them what they did specifically to launch a successful online campaign. Be prepared to take lots of notes and follow their advice. The expert I found was Joe Vitale, who educated me on the steps to take to launch a successful e-mail campaign. I strongly recommend that you follow exactly the suggestions and recommendations of the people who have already achieved the results that you want. This way you can't go wrong. You may have to invest a bit of money, but your investment will be returned multiplied.

2. Put together an irresistible offer and have a quality product. Find a number of valuable and complementary products (they can be "e" products) to give away to your customers. Make sure that your product will deliver everything you promise.

3. Have a compelling and irresistible sales letter. This is a crucial step, so it's important that you recognize where you have strengths and where you do not. If you are not good at writing sales letters, then invest some money and hire someone who is. The sales letter is one of the most critical components to the online campaign, so if you are not qualified to write it, hire an expert.

4. Line up your e-mail distribution lists. Find the people who are already reaching your audience. (You must know who your audience is before you begin this step.) Contact the list owners and ask them to help you with your campaign. Send the list owner a copy of your product and a copy of your sales letter for review. Please do not send spam under any circumstances.

5. Test, test, test. Create a seamless process for ordering. Ensure that you have tested your ordering process many times before launching your online campaign. Step through it over and over and over again. Make it easy for people to buy, and give them all of the instructions they need.

6. Be honest and ethical at *all* times. Never, ever try to take advantage of anyone. If you make a promise, follow through with everyone that you have dealings with.

7. Be responsive to customers and prospective customers. Take care of your customers; be ready to answer any questions, and respond to people's challenges as they arise. Deliver outstanding customer service.

When you create a seamless experience for your customers and provide a superior product, you will be astounded at the opportunities that an online marketing campaign will create for you. Not only can you do well financially, you will also experience exponential benefits.

The effects of the success of my first online campaign still continue. As a result of it, three foreign publishers have requested the rights to print my books. A network marketing company has brought me aboard as its corporate personal development official trainer. I've

gained a tremendous following, launched a number of other successful campaigns, and sold hundreds of copies of my second and third
books. And my own e-mail list multiplied twentyfold.

I'm firmly convinced that anyone armed with the proper tools can
achieve phenomenal success. From the moment I decided to launch my
first online campaign until the day of the launch, I invested two weeks
getting ready. This is not a huge investment of time to earn over $30,000
in 48 hours. And when you've done it once, you have the formula to repeat the campaign again and again. I wish you great success!

Peggy McColl is the author of On Being . . . The Creator of Your Destiny,
The 8 Proven Secrets to SMART Success, *and* On Being a Dog with a
Bone. *Learn more at www.destinies.com.*

35

Easy Money for Newbies at eBay

Mark Joyner

Probably the easiest way for a newbie to make some profit is to auction something off at eBay.

Everyone has something at their house that they don't need or want anymore but that might be very valuable to someone else. Auctioning things at eBay will not only help draw some money out of thin air, but it will also provide a fun laboratory where you can experiment with different sales approaches.

Here's the six-step plan:

1. Pick 40 of your items to auction. I don't care how silly or seemingly worthless they are. The items should range from the obviously valuable to the rare, the odd, and the things only a mother could love. If the items are books, limit yourself to 30 and pick 10 other items. I don't care if you select an eggbeater. In fact, one of your items should be something you're sure no one would buy.

2. Go to eBay.com and sign up to become an eBay seller.

3. Start reading some books about copywriting, marketing, and sales. There are many wonderful books out there, but remember that it's all just theory until you get out into the street and sell.

4. Create eBay pages to sell every one of those 40 products.

5. Your mission: Do *whatever it takes* to sell those items. Experiment. Try crazy things. Apply what you're reading in those books. If it's an eggbeater, give it a special spin. What's special about this eggbeater? If it's not worth much, try to find some value in it ("My great aunt said that nothing she's ever cooked with this eggbeater ever went wrong") and charge accordingly. Experiment with that price—and I don't just mean lowering it!

6. Take notice of what items sell quickly and what items are hard to sell.

With this process, you'll make some quick bucks, and you'll learn some invaluable lessons about marketing that no book could ever teach you.

Mark Joyner is the co-founder of the Guerrilla Marketing Network and a best-selling author. He can be reached at MindControlMarketing.com.

36

Two Profitable Ideas

Blair Warren

Since most newcomers to the online world will start out by establishing web sites rather than using e-mail discussion groups, autoresponders, and such, my advice is directed toward web sites. In this regard, here are two ideas that can lead to more effective and more profitable web sites for anyone just getting started online.

First, ignore the overwhelming urge to focus all your attention on the look and feel of your web site. Too many newcomers get distracted from what is really important and focus on developing sites that glitter with flashing graphics, drop down menus, multimedia presentations, and color-coordinated text and backgrounds, yet utterly lack any personality and passion.

Rather than trying to look like an Internet giant, capitalize on the fact that you are small and that you aren't slick. How? By demonstrating that you aren't a faceless corporate giant, but instead are a bona fide individual or small company that has a real passion for the product or service you offer. You do this not through fancy technology, but through good, old-fashioned copy.

And second, don't rely solely on your web site to do your sales job. While developing a fully automatic web site is certainly possible, don't make this your immediate goal when first starting out.

Instead, incorporate other forms of media into your online sales pitch. Invite people to write you and ask for a hard copy of your sales materials, which you will snail-mail to them. List a telephone number they can call to either speak with someone or listen to a prerecorded message. Tell them how they can get additional information about your product or service in stores, books, through personal references, or other off-line sources.

Why use these methods when it would be easier to e-mail your materials or have them listen to an online audio file? Because these methods help establish a sense of credibility in an environment where spam, scams, and hype reign supreme. By establishing contact with people using more personable and traditional media, the implied message is that you aren't a fly-by-night operation that might vanish tomorrow. This is a message that can mean the difference between success and failure, not only for newcomers, but for anyone who has an online presence.

Sure, use the Internet to attract the attention of those in the high-tech world, but never forget that even the most technologically advanced consumer is still a flesh-and-blood human being who prefers to do business with other flesh-and-blood human beings.

Blair Warren is the author of the book The Forbidden Keys to Persuasion. He's at www.BlairWarren.com.

37

Tell a Story in Your Subject Line

Mark Levy

I'm not an Internet guru, but I am a guy who knows how to make writing exciting. And this is what I'm willing to bet: If you write your e-mail subject lines as if they were news release headlines, you'll create more interest in your offering.

Take a look at these headlines from my own news releases:

➤ "Man Prepares to Stop Midtown Traffic with His Mind"
➤ "Author Takes a Bath in His Own Books"
➤ "Betrayal Experts to Speak to Local Business Leaders"
➤ "How to Stab a Fork in Your Eye (and Why You'd Want To)"

I think you'll agree that if you saw these pop up on your screen, you'd be curious as to the story behind them. Why? Three reasons:

1. Each paints an odd, active image.
2. Each demands that the recipient continue reading to learn more about the oddity.
3. Each stays away from making an outlandish claim about money.

Of course, if you use this tactic of writing your subject line as if it were a headline, you'll have to play fair. That is, don't use some intriguing headline, and then follow it with body copy that has nothing to do with the headline. That'll get your message opened but deleted in a heartbeat.

Instead, find the drama in your story, write a headline about it, and use the body copy of your message to continue the story. Then, and only then, tastefully make your offer to the reader—at the end, after you've delivered on your promise of a good, on-point story.

Mark Levy wrote the book Accidental Genius: Revolutionize Your Thinking through Private Writing, *which Tom Peters calls "extraordinary" and Jay Conrad Levinson calls "the very best book I have ever read on the real art of writing." Mark can be reached at www.levyinnovation.com.*

37

The Human Side of Ad Tracking

Jeff Mulligan

Do you know why people buy from you? What part of your offer put them over the edge? Let's face it, you worked for a long time on your sales copy. You created bonuses, designed a guarantee, and sweated over the benefits and how to communicate them. But which of those factors really connected with the buyers? What actually motivated the purchase? If you knew, you could pump up the benefits and the parts of your offer that really drive sales. But how can you tell?

Actually, it's very easy. You just ask. I do it every day—and it takes me virtually no time or effort to get unbelievable information. How? I add a simple e-mail to my autoresponder series immediately after a customer purchases.

Here's a sample e-mail request I might use:

Hi {firstname},

It's Jeff here, from CBmall.

I'm doing a bit of market research.

Can you tell me how you found out about CBmall? Was it a newsletter? ad? search engine? Do you remember who referred you?

Or perhaps you were reading *10 Powerful Ways CBmall Makes You Money*?

And what specifically made you decide to make the investment? What was the benefit that put you over the edge and turned you into a buyer?

This is important, because soon you will be sending traffic to the mall and this may help the CBmall sales information get better. Which will help you make more money!

Please just reply to this e-mail with the answers.

Thanks so much for your help,

Jeff Mulligan

CBmall.com

Every day these e-mails go out, and every day I get valuable information. To me, finding out why people buy is more important than why they don't (although I try to find that out, too). There are too many reasons a person may not buy, many of which are beyond my control. But knowing what turns buyers on is a huge benefit to me as I fine-tune the copy. For example, here are some of the comments I get:

➤ "I read all the info and I liked the fact that I did not have to create a web site and a bunch of other stuff. I am new to Internet marketing as well as being technically illiterate, but I figure I can follow instructions for the most part, and you offer the support I will need."

➤ "Personalized autoresponder and newsletter."

➤ "Reason: The e-book *10 Powerful Ways CBmall Makes You Money* made good marketing sense. . . . Also the products on ClickBank-CBmall are terrific and good sellers. . . ."

➤ "I found your ad at clickbank.com."

➤ "I first heard of CBmall from your newsletter, which I sub-scribed to in December, but was not convinced. My next step was to get the *10 Powerful Ways CBmall Makes You Money.* This made things much clearer. The number of products available is impressive. The targeted traffic that is shared among own-ers is a useful bonus. The guarantee means no risk, which is essential as I am on a small pension."

■ WHAT YOU CAN LEARN

Let's look at this small sample to see what I can learn from it.

➤ My ad on the ClickBank web site is working—keep it going.

➤ I have a lot of beginners who don't have a web site of their own. I should continue to highlight this feature.

➤ People like the fact that there is a built-in autoresponder that puts their affiliate links on all the messages that go out. It means they get multiple chances to sell. Perhaps I should pro-mote this more.

➤ My e-book and e-course, *10 Powerful Ways CBmall Makes You Money,* is working.

➤ Look at the last message. This is evidence of how important follow-up is. This person waited three months before she felt comfortable ordering.

➤ The guarantee is very important.

While I can only show you a small sample here, there are many more that echo these thoughts. Put them together and you can see clear trends about what features come up most frequently. For me, ease of use, the ClickBank affiliation, and the personalized autore-sponders are the most common reasons people buy. I have adjusted the sales copy to highlight these features.

Note for ClickBank affiliates: If you use ClickBank, you know that you get the e-mail address of your customers. You can use that to send a quick e-mail requesting this information.

A word about timing: I have found that this works really well if you send the e-mail out immediately after the purchase. Mine goes out at the same time the thank you e-mail goes out. This way, the reasons are still fresh in the customer's mind, and they are in a very cooperative mood—often quite excited from their purchase and anxious to do anything to help.

How to reply: I set up a simple macro so that I can just hit reply, activate the macro, and hit send. It just takes a few seconds. Mine says simply, "Thank you for helping out with your input. I really appreciate it. I look forward to helping you make extra money with your new CBmall." That's all you need—but you should be sure to acknowledge their answers with a reply.

■ HOW THIS HELPS YOUR AFFILIATE PROGRAM

Here's another great fringe benefit of this tactic. Often customers will specifically mention the newsletter they were reading or the web site they were visiting that first told them about CBmall. When they do, I will frequently copy the e-mail and send it to that newsletter or web site owner. Since these people are my affiliates, it's a great way to show them how their CBmall promotions are working. It also shows them I am paying attention to their business. Remember that mind share is important in keeping your affiliates active and promoting your products. I've garnered considerable goodwill through these quick little messages.

■ SUMMARY

In summary, while ad tracking is vital to learn *where* your business is coming from, an autoresponder message to find out *why* you got your business is often just as valuable. Implement this simple tactic and give yourself a better understanding of what is working for you. Use that knowledge to fine-tune your site for maximum conversions.

Jeff Mulligan has an MBA and 20-plus years of marketing experience as an ad agency senior VP and VP of marketing for two software companies. Jeff owns CBmall, a site that provides 10 different ways for ClickBank affiliates to earn income on 1,997 ClickBank InfoProducts. Find out more at http://www.cbmall.com/info.

39

How to Create a Simple Internet Marketing Business Plan for Maximum Profits—Part 1

Terry Dean

You may not be seeking a business loan, but that doesn't mean you don't need an Internet marketing business plan. Too many people just jump from idea to idea—and product to product. Every week they think they've found the new Holy Grail of online marketing. Hot opportunities come up every week, along with the newest advertising trends. The ads scream, "Just do this and you'll be a millionaire!" So Joe Blow immediately dumps what he's been doing and jumps on the new bandwagon. I've heard it a thousand times: "I've got an awesome feeling about this one!" Next week he finds out that feeling was just indigestion.

Let me state this as emphatically as I can: Making money online is a *business*. It's not just an opportunity, and it's not about paying someone else to do all the work for you. If you want to hand someone else your cash and wait for them to make you rich, then stand in line. A lot of people are willing to take your money. But after you've given your money, you'll wait a *long* time before you get any results.

Don't think for a minute that I'm putting down business training. That's what my business does. What I'm putting down is an attitude that there's one secret you can learn that will immediately make you successful—to the exclusion of everything else you need to learn. You may learn something that immediately doubles or triples your profits (one change in an ad can do that). But if you refuse to learn anything else, you're in trouble.

One of my favorite comparisons to online marketing is college. You go to college to increase your earning power. That's the same thing you need to do in your online business. Study, learn what works and what doesn't, and your earning power increases. The good news is you can learn online marketing a whole lot quicker than four years—and your income potential is much higher than with a bachelor's degree in anything. But rarely do you earn money overnight.

When you go away to college, you don't sign up for only one class and that's it. You don't just say, "Hey professor, tell me the secret to being a brain surgeon. And make it quick. I only have an hour before my favorite TV show comes on." It's the same way with online marketing. Don't read just one e-book and think you know everything there is to know about marketing. Don't listen to just one audiotape. Learn the entire system for earning big profits. Then practice . . . practice . . . practice.

The most successful marketers are also the best students. They constantly study, read, listen, and watch. They go to conferences. They brainstorm with other marketers. They then test and put into practice what they've learned.

I spend around $10,000 per year on information products including books, e-books, audiotapes, videos, teleconferences, and more. One of the richest marketers I work with spends $35,000 or more per year on his education. You don't have to spend that much starting out, but you should plan and budget something for educational expenses. You also have to budget money for web hosting, autoresponders, and advertising. The minimum I usually tell people to budget for their business and online education is $100 a month, although it's much easier if you have more to work with.

It's the same with your time. Since almost everyone starts out part-time in their Internet business, you have very limited time to work with. You're going to have to sacrifice something to make time for your business. You may have to give up TV. You may even have to give up a little sleep.

If you don't *plan* to succeed, then circumstances will plan for your failure.

■ SET GOALS FOR YOUR NEXT TWELVE MONTHS

I was very bad at goal setting when I first started my business, and I've come to find out that most of my customers are making big mistakes in this area as well. You have to set goals for your online business. If you don't know where you're going, then how do you ever plan to get there?

Most people simply say they want to make $5,000 a month and quit their job. That's not enough. Be more specific. What would you like your life to be like a year from now? How about 5 years from now? How about 20 years? Where would you like to live? How much do you want to earn each year? How would you like to spend your time? Do you want to travel or stay home? Do you want more time to spend going to your kid's Little League games? Would you like to pay off the mortgage on your current home, or move to a nicer one? Would you like to work mornings so you can spend your afternoons at the golf course? What kind of car do you want to drive? How much do you plan to save each year? How much do you want in your bank account? How much do you want to be able to give away to good works? In other words, paint a specific picture for your life.

For your Internet business, we'll focus on your next 12 months, but you should first look further into the future to get an idea of your long-term goals. Then, once you have figured them out, back up to 12 months from now. Planning an Internet business for the next 20 years is next to impossible. The Internet changes at warp speed—and you have no idea what it will even look like five years from now. So the easiest way to focus is to concentrate only on the next 12 months for your Internet business.

What is life going to be like 12 months from now? Sure, it won't be as grand as your eventual goals. And it probably won't include you being a multi-millionaire yet. But if you create a successful Internet business it can be quite different from the lifestyle you're living today. So how would you like to be living 12 months from now?

■ PLAN YOUR MONTHLY, WEEKLY, AND DAILY ACTIONS TO REACH YOUR GOALS

Having a set of goals won't do you an ounce of good if you don't come up with a practical plan for reaching those goals. This is where many people turn their backs on self-help authors. You can have incredible goals, but if you don't take daily steps toward them, you'll never realize them.

Let's say, for example, that one of your goals is to earn $5,000 net profit per month from your Internet business 12 months from now. If expenses such as affiliate commissions, hosting, advertising, product delivery, and so on, take up half your income, then you're really looking at making $10,000 per month gross profit.

Earning $5,000 a month in net profit 12 months from now is not an unrealistic goal at all. If you put in a little time each day you shouldn't have much trouble reaching that point in 12 months. In fact, if you were to work hard, you should be able to get there a lot faster, or even be earning a lot more money in this time frame.

Now take that goal and figure out what steps you need to take to get there. What do you need to accomplish each month for the next 12 months to reach that goal? If you're starting from scratch and want to focus on an information business, then your 12-month plan may look something like this:

➤ Month 1: Study potential niche markets. Find frustrations and wants not being fulfilled in the marketplace. Find out what the market's hot buttons are (the things that make them buy one product over another).

➤ Month 2: Decide on a product. Create a web site and work on the rough draft of a sales letter for your soon-to-be product. Start building an opt-in e-mail list of prospects in your target market.

➤ Month 3: Create your first product (usually an e-book or audiotape) and finish preparing the sales material for it. Be sure to refer people to affiliate links throughout it for additional income. Sell it to the prospect list you've been building for the last month. Earn $200 net profit.

➤ Month 4: Test "pay-per-click" (PPC) search engine advertising and e-zine advertising extensively for your new product offer. Write several articles for submission to e-zines. See if you can increase the conversion rates with a different headline, price, or bonus. Earn $300 net profit.

➤ Month 5: Start an affiliate program. Create banners, solo ads, classified ads, endorsements, and the like. Provide all the tools your new affiliates will need to promote the program. Earn $500 net profit.

➤ Month 6: Spend the month looking for top affiliates, e-zine publishers, and e-book authors. Offer them increased commissions to be part of your program. Earn at least $1,000 net profit this month from their endorsements.

➤ Month 7: Continue the process of looking for top affiliates this month. Your goal is to make bigger deals and get in larger publications. Earn $2,000 net profit this month.

➤ Month 8: Start working on your first back-end product. You should have begun to receive feedback on this product. Look through e-mails you've received and find other frustrations your customers are coming up against. Use this material for your second product. Continue to earn $2,000 net profit from your first product.

➤ Month 9: Keep promoting your first product and finding new affiliates. At the same time, complete your new product and sales piece. Your goal is to be able to earn the same income of $2,000 net profit even though your attention is on a new product.

➤ Month 10: Offer this second product to your prospect and customer list. Plug it into your current affiliate program. Send out e-mails to all of your affiliates to promote this product also. Your goal is $5,000 in net profit this month from the two products.

➤ Month 11: Prepare a complete e-mail follow-up system for both products. Have any customer who buys one immediately start receiving information on the other one. Start testing advanced forms of marketing such as banners, co-registrations, post-cards, and so forth. Your goal this month is $3,000 in net profit because of increased ad expenses, but you also expect to have completed another automated advertising income source.

➤ Month 12: Continue all of the working advertising such as e-zines, PPC search engines, and anything else proven to work. Continually motivate your affiliates. Start planning for your third related product in this market. Your goal is $5,000 net profit from mostly automated sources.

■ BREAK YOUR PLAN DOWN INTO DAILY TASKS

As you can see, the plan so far is not complete. It is only a basic outline of a 12-month goal. What you would do next is break up the months and separate them into weekly goals. What do you want to accomplish each week in your online business to reach your monthly goals? I've proven it to myself again and again: Even though I know how to make good money using Internet marketing for any product or service, I will still accomplish at least twice as much each week when I've written down my goals.

I even break my weekly goals down into daily tasks. Then I examine how much I've accomplished at the end of each day to prepare a quick task list for the next day. This isn't advanced time management. It's just a simple way I do things for maximum effectiveness in my business—and it causes many people to ask how I can accomplish so much in the little amount of time I work.

Whenever I don't plan in this way, I end up wasting too much precious time checking e-mails 10 times a day or reading unimportant web sites. I'll lose two to three hours without even noticing, when I'm not focused in my daily plans. So once you have outlined your monthly and weekly goals, break them down into the specific tasks you need to accomplish each day in order to achieve the longer-term goals.

Caution: Most people will overestimate how much they can accomplish in a week, and underestimate how much they'll accomplish in a year. I've had a lot of people tell me they have to make $10,000 by next week. When I ask about assets, they don't have a product, a web site, a list, or any relationships with people who do have those things.

If you had an irresistible product and sales letter, then you could potentially make $10,000 in a week through a relationship with a list owner. If you owned an e-mail list, it would be easy to create that kind of overnight money with the right product. If you had strong relationships with other marketers, you could combine list owners with product owners and do it without any hard asset. The only problem is that these relationships take time to build; the biggest windfall profits almost always occur after you've proven yourself to these people time and time again.

Still, some people actually believe they can earn $10,000 with a few hours of work, with no contacts or assets and no experience whatsoever. If it were that easy, everybody would be doing it. Yet those same people have trouble believing in a plan like the one I laid out earlier. They're so busy looking for the quick buck that they can't see long-term residual income from taking the right steps. They don't believe they can do the things I've outlined.

You can achieve your goals if you break them down into smaller monthly, weekly, and daily tasks. Even if you only have a few hours a week to work, you can still make it work. Just plan a couple of little tasks to accomplish each day. Then force yourself to do them regardless of how you feel that day. Do it every day, and within 12 months you could own your own automatic Internet money machine.

■ WHAT ABOUT THE BIG MONEY?

Nothing I have said thus far has been intended to discourage you—only to try to set you on a practical success plan. You may do everything I've recommended and hit the market just right with a big winner that starts earning huge profits immediately.

Statistics show that the average large corporation only hits a big winner on one out of seven tries. But you don't need a huge winner online to make good money (in other words, you don't need 1,000,000 customers). Almost every client I work with has a profitable project—it just isn't always a home run.

The plan I've outlined is based on you creating a successful product on your first try, though not necessarily a home run project. If your product offer is perfect for the marketplace and it's something people have been frustrated about and waiting for, you could end up earning $30,000, $50,000, or more the first month it's released. This would happen because the market has a demand that hasn't been satisfied and your offer hits them perfectly with both the product and the sales piece.

Just don't set yourself up to fail by feeling you *have* to create a huge winner. Yes, you can find a few success stories about people who have done it, but I can show you a lot more people who've lost while playing a high-risk game like this. I've seen a lot of people who hear about those big immediate successes and expect every business to work exactly like that. This hurts them badly because they never set up a realistic plan to follow in case it doesn't happen. You're much better off setting up a 12-month plan and following it. Then when the big winner hits, you ride it and change your plan accordingly.

In Part 2 (Chapter 39), I'll use the 12-month plan to demonstrate an advanced Internet marketer's goals and plans—including how to use lifestyle considerations and marketing. Plus you'll see a second beginner's Internet marketing plan.

Terry Dean, a five-year veteran of Internet marketing, will take you by the hand and show you exact results of all the marketing techniques he tests. See www.netbreakthroughs.com.

40

How to Create a Simple Internet Marketing Business Plan for Maximum Profits—Part 2

Terry Dean

In Chapter 38 we saw the importance of establishing goals and plans. This chapter continues that subject, but I want to take a little detour in it. Instead of talking specifically about the plans you should be making, I want to show you part of my own business plan for the next year. This can and should give you some ideas for your own planning. Keep in mind that I've been doing this for years now and am working at it full-time, so the number of projects I want to accomplish will be higher than for the average person who is just starting out.

■ USE THE INTERNET TO CREATE THE LIFESTYLE OF YOUR DREAMS

Let's talk directly about your Internet business. I've taught people many times that you need to find something you'd enjoy doing in order to create a successful online business, but let's go even deeper than that. Hopefully your life is about more than just money. Yes, you can make a lot of money online. You can do it very quickly in many cases as well. But I personally refuse to give up my life, my family, or my health in search of the almighty dollar.

If your goal was to earn as much as humanly possible and nothing else mattered, then you could sit there working twelve hours a day, seven days a week. Doing so could yield a huge increase in your in-come over the short term—until you lost your health or the rest of your life. I'm just not willing to do that, and hopefully you aren't either.

Besides limiting the amount of time I work to a maximum (it's very rare for me to ever work more than forty hours in one week), I've also woven other lifestyle considerations into my future planning. I'll name a few of them and how they apply to my business.

➤ No Employees

Employees can give you a measure of leverage and help you earn more in less time by multiplying yourself. That's the positive side. The negative side is they also require a lot of hand-holding and watching over. If you have a lot of employees, you'll end up spending as much time watching over them as you do getting any real work done.

So I've chosen to go without employees. I'll hire outside freelancers, like transcriptionists, tape duplicators, fulfillment sources, and programmers, when I need them. I just don't want to have any of them on the payroll. My business consists of my wife and me—and it will continue this way over the next year.

➤ Limited Phone Contact

I'm a very shy person by nature. When you stick me in a group of people I may never speak at all. While strong person-to-person sales skills could possibly increase my overall profits, I hate working that way. So I avoid doing any kind of direct selling over the phone.

You'll also find that my web sites don't list my phone number in an obvious area. This is because when I used to provide it, I received more calls for free advice than for orders. Even when I used an outside order-taking service, they received 10 times as many calls of people leaving a message for me to call them as they did orders. Having a phone number actually hurt my sales because of the freebie seekers in my market. I'm not saying this is true for everyone. Most businesses will find that putting their phone number in a very obvious area will increase sales because of credibility. And you can get an outside order-taking service such as http://www.customerdirect.com to take the incoming calls.

➤ Consistent Monthly Income

I've received both kinds of income: big one-time bursts of cash flow and residual monthly income. A high-ticket product release will often give me an immediate jump in income by $30,000 to $100,000. If you plan for big product launches and set up a number of joint ventures for them, you can get this kind of instant cash flow online.

But I prefer the monthly income I get from a membership site. It is reliable income that comes in every single month. It's also a slightly different kind of work. When you go for a quick burst of income, you focus on a lot of work short term (creating the offer and the product, setting up joint ventures, tracking, etc.). With a membership site, the work is spread out over a long time. You do a little today, a little tomorrow, and so on. Instead of a quick burst of work, it's done over time. Best of all, residual income is reliable income.

➤ Low Overhead

My business is based on low overhead. I don't have any employees and I keep business bills to a minimum (everything is paid for up front when possible). My dedicated server running all my sites is my most expensive bill, at around $400 a month. When you add up all my required expenses, it is less than $1,000 a month—in a highly profitable business.

Plus, since I sell information products, my product expenses are low. My biggest monthly expenses are my affiliates and advertising. And affiliates are only getting paid if they're making sales, so they're risk-free. My net profits are usually just over half of my overall gross profits, and most of what goes out goes to affiliates. This all produces a very secure and comfortable income for me.

➤ Writing

My favorite part of business is the research and writing aspect. That's what I enjoy doing most, so I've based my business on doing a lot of it. Because of its setup and sections, Netbreakthroughs requires a lot of research and writing. If I enjoyed a different aspect of my business the most, then I would have chosen a different setup.

It could have focused more on doing interviews. It could have been based on resources. It could have been based on video training. It could have been focused on teleconferences. It could have been based on monthly marketing tools. There are dozens of ways to do a membership site, but I chose mine based on my lifestyle choice: What did I want to do?

➤ Limited Travel

I like to travel a little bit, but not too much. Dealing with airlines once a month is enough for me, so I only speak at a few conferences each year. The travel and hassle just wears me out too much to want to focus on it. Getting out and meeting my customers live, though, does help give me a stronger focus to my business. And the networking that takes place at the conferences is probably the biggest benefit of all (okay, the income from speaking is decent also).

While professional speaking can be used to produce a very high income (some speakers with good product sales skills can earn more than a million a year), it just isn't something I'd want to do. Being on the road 200 days a year would be a nightmare for me. So very limited speaking fits into my personal lifestyle plan.

➤ Long Weekends

Rather than take a few long vacations, I prefer to take short three- or four-day weekends at regular intervals. Sometimes I'll spend it at home riding all-terrain vehicles in the woods and relaxing by the fireplace. Other times I purchase a last-minute vacation at one of the online travel sites and travel to Colorado, Florida, or elsewhere for an adventure like mountain biking or sailing.

I've simply built these breaks into my business model. If you prefer month-long vacations three times a year, you need to build that into your plan. You may want to work a year and then take a whole year off. If so, build that into your business plan. (Hint: You would want to focus on creating a sellable business that you could build during the year and then sell out.)

■ GENERATE MULTIPLE STREAMS OF INCOME FROM ONE GROUP OF CUSTOMERS

Thinking about the kind of lifestyle you want to create is only part of your business planning. You also need to plan for earning multiple streams of income from the same group of customers.

Thirty years ago, a business could get away with only having one low-priced product, but today that's a good recipe for going broke. Your biggest expense in any business will always be the cost of generating a new customer. It may cost you $40 in advertising or other expenses to generate a $50 sale. As you expand your business and take on more expensive advertising, it may even cost you $75 to generate that $50 sale.

You have to make a second sale, a third sale, and a fourth sale to those same customers. That's where the profits are. Always think of your first product as a lead generator. It's the *start* of your relationship with a customer, not the conclusion. You don't just make a sale and go off in search of more customers. You make a sale and then begin your relationship.

Take a look at my multiple streams of income and my plans for the next year.

➤ Web Gold

This is my free newsletter at http://www.bizpromo.com. It is published twice monthly. It is the catalyst for selling my other products and services. I earn instant money-on-demand every time I send out an issue. I've even used it to generate over $70,000 in a single e-mail offer. This is why I focus so much on the list. Build the list and earn profits from it forever. Every one of my other products is offered through my newsletter for maximum profits (and multiple income streams).

➤ Affiliate Programs

I always earn more money when I offer my own products and services in my newsletter, but I simply don't create a new product twice every month. So I also offer other people's products through affiliate programs and joint ventures. I currently receive at least 15 different checks each month from affiliate programs. Another great place to make affiliate offers is inside my products themselves.

By finding quality resources with affiliate programs attached, you can install 10 to 20 automatic streams of income in an e-book or any other product you create. If you don't offer further resources in your products, you're leaving a lot of money on the table. The majority of my affiliate income comes through these product mentions.

➤ Netbreakthroughs

My monthly membership is my largest residual income. I like receiving checks, so I have my processor set to send me two large checks per month. Although Netbreakthroughs takes more work than any of my other projects or products, it's worth it because of the constant residual income I receive.

Having your own membership site has a second purpose you may never have thought of. It helps you to build a strong relationship with your customers. My Netbreakthroughs members are some of my best customers, purchasing multiple other products and services from me. By constantly providing new content and information for your customers, you'll build this stronger bond and make more back-end sales of other products and services.

➤ E-Books

Digital products are a nice profit center, so I will continue to offer a few e-books such as *Paperless Newsletter* and a couple of others. All is not great in digital land, though. None of my main future products are planned in e-book format. There are so many e-books in the marketing field that they have lost an incredible amount of perceived value. There have been too many poor e-books published, and people are pricing them so cheap that they've lost their value.

This trend has not affected other niches yet, so there are still huge opportunities in e-book publishing outside of marketing subjects. I would not recommend anyone publish e-books in the marketing niche as a primary profit center anymore. New e-books are not part of my future business.

➤ Books

During the next year I will be releasing my first book in paperback format. While e-books on marketing have lost their perceived value, paperback books have continued to prove extremely valuable. Having your own book immediately sets you apart as an expert. Tell people you're an author, and you gain an aura of credibility. Tell them you're an e-book author and it means nothing to them.

The selling of the book itself doesn't produce a lot of profits. At a cost of $19.95, you're not going to earn much. The purpose of the book isn't for the immediate profits. It's for the back-end sales that come out of it. It's also for the credibility and additional open doors it gives you to market (such as publicity and seminars). I have one book planned over the next 12 months.

➤ Tape Sets

I resisted doing tape sets for a while because of surveys I've done. Every time I do a survey online, the results indicate that people prefer e-books to tape sets. This held me back from offering tape sets for quite a while. Once I started offering them, though, I took an immediate jump in sales. People love the tape sets. Many customers e-mail me to tell me that they've listened to a set many times until they literally wore the tapes out.

Offering tape sets also gives me the opportunity to include inserts in the package for other tape sets and other offers. A good percentage of the customers immediately buy another offer. So the tape sets have been giving me increased back-end sales over digital offers. For people who like the immediate gratification of e-books, I offer a transcript of the tapes for immediate digital delivery as a bonus.

All the surveys prove is that people who respond to surveys don't like tapes. People who have money do like tapes. People vote with their wallets, not their opinions.

I have three more tape sets planned on specific subjects over the next 3 months; a total of six are scheduled for the next 12 months. A couple will be done by teleseminar.

➤ Videos and DVDs

Video is an awesome way to deliver information—and with a DVD you can pack in three hours of video plus bonus materials. You can deliver limited video online in short bursts, but you always have technical difficulty with some customers. If you put the same video on DVD, you won't have the technical issues and you'll have a higher perceived value along with top-notch quality.

A screencam video can be done with Camtasia at http://www.techsmith.com. Then use simple DVD creation tools such as the DVD workshop software at http://www.ulead.com. DVDs can be duplicated for $2 to $3 apiece once finished. I have two DVD-only projects scheduled, and my next workshop will be taped for DVD format over the next 12 months.

➤ Workshops

There's nothing quite like a live workshop for relationship building and networking. While I will continue to do a few speaking engagements, I am also planning for at least one training workshop over the next year. It will be on a specific subject of Internet marketing (such as copywriting, joint ventures, affiliate programs, list building, etc.) and will be a high-ticket item with only 20 to 30 people allowed in attendance. The price will be $3,000 or more.

Some customers learn best in a group environment like this. The workshop will give me the opportunity to teach advanced information in a small group format that offers lots of personal support. It will generate a nice income—and allow me to produce a set of videos and DVDs.

➤ Coaching

Customers love personal coaching programs. They receive all the information they need to learn, plus they get personal assistance with their questions. So coaching sells very easily. The big disadvantages of coaching programs are that you can only serve a limited number of clients and it is time intensive.

The best coaching approach I've found is to do group teleconferences along with e-mail consultations. This gives you the best of both worlds. You bond and do the training during the teleconferences. Then you do the one-on-one support at your convenience through e-mail. Although I've seen some people do e-classes only (with only e-mail support), that doesn't generate the same level of success for your customers. From what I've seen and heard, the percentage of customers who actually use an e-class only is a very small number. They just don't get motivated to do their assignments without the live interaction of the teleconference.

I will continue to run a coaching program, accepting only a small group of customers at one time.

➤ Multiple Streams of Income

The beauty of all the preceding products is that they are sold to the same group of customers. Even when I place an ad and seemingly lose the money I spent on it, I still usually win from back-end selling. It's rare that I truly lose on any ad.

You're basically building a funnel system. A huge number of people purchase your low-cost items, such as an e-book or book. They then purchase an audiotape set. Higher-level packages are offered along with videos or DVDs, and some of your customers purchase those. A workshop or coaching program may only get 30 sales, but it has zero cost of advertising since all the people seeing the ad are already customers. All the different streams of income add to your bottom line and produce a widely successful online business.

■ YOUR BUSINESS IS ALL ABOUT MARKETING

No matter how many great products and services you offer, it still comes down to the marketing. You have to constantly market your business to be successful. That's your primary business purpose—marketing. What follows are some of the techniques I'm focusing on to grow my personal business.

➤ Affiliates

Affiliates who have their own e-zines or publish their own products can generate a lot of sales for my products and services. So I'm making targeting these super-affiliates a primary goal for the next year. I will pay a freelancer to help search out and contact these people for selling all of my products and services. The goal will be to find and sign up at least five new super-affiliates per week. The only costs will be the freelancer's wages along with the commissions I pay to the affiliates themselves.

➤ PPC Search Engines

Google, Overture, and other PPC search engines will continue to be a primary advertising tool for me, although their importance will be dropping slightly as I pay more attention to other forms of advertising, such as banner ads and off-line marketing. I will continue to test the different PPC search engines to find ones which are worth your time and mine to use for advertising.

➤ Opt-In E-Mail Advertising

Opt-in e-mail advertising is still a big portion of my ad budget. I regularly advertise in e-zines and have been testing other opt-in services as well. The big disadvantage of opt-in e-mail is that a good ad can only run two to three times in an e-zine before it loses its effectiveness. So you have to constantly seek out new e-zines to place ads in.

While this will continue to be a primary advertising method for me over the next year, I use it in bursts. When I find an ad that works, I run it in a large number of e-zines that I've already tested, all at the same time. Then I search out other e-zines over time to slowly run test ads in.

➤ Other Online Ad Formats

If it's easy, everyone will soon be doing it. That's why PPC search engine advertising has gotten so expensive. So I'm constantly on the lookout for other forms of online marketing outside the norm.

What I'm looking for specifically are forms of advertising where it's easy to expand to high numbers of ads. This is one of the reasons I've been testing a lot of banner advertising lately. There are lots of places to buy banners, so this can be very powerful when it has been proven to work for you. I'll also be testing other forms of online advertising in the future.

➤ Off-Line Marketing

A lot of Internet marketers have neglected off-line marketing—including me. Other than using postcards, I've done little off-line marketing. Over the next year I'll be doing more postcard mailings to purchased lists, along with sales letter mailings to my own customer lists. I will also be testing a few display ads in magazines, postcard decks, and other forms of off-line marketing over the next year. The advantage of off-line marketing is that it's often easier to expand and reach large audiences when you have a successful ad.

➤ Conferences

I will continue to do a few conferences next year, and I consider this a marketing medium. I speak and pull in new clients. Although the number of clients I receive from conferences is low compared to the number of online clients I have, these are often the clients who are willing to buy the higher-ticket items. So a low number of them can be quite profitable.

Plus, just being at the conferences always provides networking opportunities. We make friendships and deals with other serious marketers. A single conference can produce 10 or more joint ventures with other top businesses.

■ ANOTHER 12-MONTH PLAN FOR BEGINNERS

No matter what lifestyle, income streams, and marketing plan you use, you have to remember that making money online is all about the *list*. So the best strategy for someone starting out is not to try to do everything I've mentioned—that's a good way to get frustrated. Remember, I'm full-time in this business and have my wife, Julie, who works part-time with me.

Make your business start-up simple. Concentrate on building a list. Find affiliate programs and joint venture partners to supply products and income. Plan your lifestyle considerations. Then put together a marketing plan you can work with.

If you want to promote affiliate programs, then your plan may look something like this:

➤ Month 1: Study potential niche markets. Find frustrations and wants not being fulfilled in the marketplace. Find out what the market's hot buttons are (the things that make them buy one product over another).

➤ Month 2: Come up with a subject for a free newsletter. Create a web site and work on a special free report or free e-course series to give away. Write several ads for it, such as a description ad for co-registration services, a solo ad, and a sponsor ad. Make sure to build affiliate links for several products or services into your series (3 to 10, depending on the subject).

➤ Month 3: Concentrate on writing your first articles and e-zine issues. Submit two articles to other e-zines. Submit them to article databases as well. Start participating in discussion boards on the topic, and constantly link your posts to your free subscription page. From now on, every e-zine issue should have information plus referrals for affiliate programs. Try to earn at least $200 from affiliate programs this month.

➤ Month 4: Sign up for one co-registration service to start sending leads. Also begin testing e-zine advertising and PPC search engine advertising. Begin trading ads with other e-zine publishers (continue this every month from now on). Because of the advertising expense this month, try to break even on your business.

➤ Month 5: Refine your PPC ads and continue to use e-zines if they are working. Submit at least two more articles this month to e-zines and article databases. Start a co-op or plan a publisher joint venture. Get five e-zine publishers to work with you to build lists (through a co-op ad or by recommending each other together). Earn $250 net profit.

➤ Month 6: Continue your advertising from previous months including the PPC ads, e-zine ads, trade ads, discussion boards, article submissions, and the co-op ads. Take all your articles and turn them into a free e-book to give away at your site (a traffic virus). Earn at least $500 net profit this month from affiliate programs.

➤ Month 7: Begin offering your free e-book along with your e-zine. Add a recommend-a-friend script for others to recommend it, and allow others to give it away free. Continue all forms of advertising you're currently using. Earn $750 net profit this month.

➤ Month 8: While continuing your normal advertising schedule, also add in a second co-op or joint venture deal to grow your lists with other publishers. Plus, concentrate on a major joint venture endorsement offer of someone else's product. Get a special discount or bonus for your subscribers and offer it multiple times to your list. Earn $3,000 net profit from affiliate programs and your endorsement.

➤ Month 9: Continue your advertising schedule. Post some of your articles to your web site. Then focus on a link campaign using software such as Zeus, available at http://www.cyber-robotics.com. Build a link directory by trading links with other web sites. This is to draw link traffic and to boost rankings in the search engines. Earn a net profit of $1,500 this month.

➤ Month 10: Continue your advertising schedule. Create your first product (usually an e-book) and work on the sales material for it. Make sure to refer people to your affiliate links throughout it for additional income. Earn a profit of $1,500 this month.

➤ Month 11: Continue your normal advertising schedule. Finish your sales copy. Offer your new product to your customer list. Earn $4,000 net profit from normal affiliate sales and the release of your new product.

➤ Month 12: Set up an affiliate program and allow all those publishers you've been doing co-ops and joint ventures with to sell your product. The relationships you've built over the past year should allow you to secure these joint ventures quickly. Earn $7,500 net profit because of the 10 e-zines that run ads for your product.

41

The Lazy Person's Quick and Easy Guide to Affiliate Success—Part 1

Terry Dean

I produced this guide in response to one of the most common questions asked by Netbreakthroughs members. A week doesn't go by without someone asking me if the information inside Netbreakthroughs will work for affiliates. In other words, do they have to have their own product to succeed online? The information inside of this membership definitely works for affiliates—and no, you don't have to have your own product to succeed online.

The reason I talk so much about creating or selling information products is because it is one of the most lucrative online businesses. It has built-in back-end selling opportunities, establishes you as an expert, and allows you to start your own affiliate program. But selling information is *not* the only way to succeed online.

Tens of thousands of affiliates earn a good income just selling other people's products or services. Some affiliates like to earn a few hundred extra dollars a month while working in the comfort of their own home. Others are out to replace their current incomes and become full-time Internet marketers. You can accomplish either goal by becoming an affiliate for other people's products.

Some people may not know what an affiliate is, so let's cover that before we get too far into the material. An affiliate is simply an individual or business who signs up to promote someone else's product or service for a share of the profits. For example, you can sign up to be an affiliate with Netbreakthroughs. You then promote this membership site, and for anyone who signs up through your link (you're given a special link so we know which customers you sent to us), you're paid a commission every single month for as long as they're a member.

The advantages of being an affiliate include those:

➤ No product development: The products are already there.

➤ No sales copywriting: The sales materials are already written.

➤ No merchant account: You don't have to process the orders.

➤ No customer service: The companies themselves usually deal with any customer problems.

All in all, being an affiliate is one of the quickest and easiest businesses to start. You can even sign up for free in the majority of programs. Refer to http://www.associateprograms.com to find a large number of potential programs for you to join.

This doesn't mean that there aren't problems with being an affiliate. There are problems. The biggest one is the fact that the great majority of affiliate program managers don't have *your* best interests at heart. In other words, they are not going to tell you everything you need to know to make yourself successful. They'll only tell you what makes them the most money—whether it works for you or not.

■ THE DECK IS STACKED AGAINST THE AVERAGE JOE

Top affiliate marketing experts tell you that only 1 out of 100 affiliates ever really does anything with the business. Yet they also rave about how much money anyone can make as an affiliate! Do you see a problem here? Having a 1 percent chance of success is not the kind of business I want to start. That's even worse than the average retail business. No thanks.

It's a good thing you don't have to accept those odds. Those odds are for the average Joe. Let me tell you how the average Joe markets the affiliate program—including his thought process. He sees an affiliate program paying 50 percent commission and his mind jumps to attention. He can make $50 off every $100 sale . . . he doesn't have to write any ads . . . and all he has to do is follow the step-by-step system already laid out for him. In other words, he doesn't even have to think either! He jumps at the chance and signs up for free.

He gets the instructions e-mailed to him from the affiliate manager. The instructions tell him to take this five-line ad and place it in e-zines. So he says, "Okay, I can afford $40 for an ad." He places the ad and one sale occurs. Good. At least he made a $10 profit. He thinks, "Hmmm, maybe that e-zine wasn't a good one." So he places two more ads, for $75 and $100. One of these ads does well and makes two sales. He earns a $25 profit (after paying $75 for the ad). The second ad only makes one sale. He lost $50 on this one (since he paid $100 for the ad). He has now made four sales and has lost a total of $15.

He gives up on this affiliate program in frustration. But he joins another affiliate program, hoping this one will be the answer. Maybe that last one just didn't sell well enough. This new affiliate program tells him to place "pay-per-click" (PPC) search engine advertising. He says, "Yes, that's the answer. They had me placing the wrong advertising!" Average Joe now spends all day coming up with keywords. He finds out that there aren't many penny opportunities out there anymore and that you have to spend 10 cents, 20 cents, or more for most of the keywords. So he ends up paying $100 the first month for click-throughs and makes three sales.

This affiliate program pays the same commission, so this adds up to $50 in profit. The same number of click-throughs occur the next month, but only two sales occur, and so average Joe just breaks even for the month.

So average Joe gives up on this affiliate program and joins a new one. This time average Joe says, "I know the secret now. I have to only use free advertising." So Joe spends 10 hours writing his first article and sends it out to e-zines. One of them runs the article and one sale occurs. Joe earns $50. The only problem is that this breaks down to only $5 an hour once you count the amount of time spent to produce this sale. Joe could have done a lot better working overtime at his job! So average Joe says "Forget it" to the whole idea. . . .

Let's take a look at what happened. Sometimes money would be made, other times money was lost. Do you notice who makes a profit no matter what happens—and never has to risk a penny? That's right. The affiliate manager makes money no matter what!

Average affiliates may earn or lose money. The affiliate manager only pays them when they generate a profit. So the affiliate manager wins on the deal whether the advertising system he writes up for his affiliates works well or not.

The deck is stacked against average affiliates. They only have a 1 percent chance of playing this game and winning.

■ THE BIG MYTH

Let's change the odds. The big myth of online affiliate programs is that someone will hand you a good income. All you have to do is sign up for free, and it's like money in the bank. Most people sense that it's a myth, but the affiliate program managers make it sound so easy sometimes.

The key to becoming a successful affiliate is to stack the deck in your favor. This will shock some people, but I'll say it anyway: The best way to succeed in an affiliate program is *not* to lead people to the product site. The best way isn't to build a mini site that leads into the product site, either. Both of those methods promote the affiliate manager—and leave you out of the profit loop.

The best way to make money in affiliate programs is to build an opt-in e-mail list and then promote one affiliate product after another to your list. The purpose of your web site is to build a list. If you're doing anything else with it, then you're missing out.

Focus on building your list and then selling the products you affiliate with. This way you become the one in control. It's *your* list. If you want to promote Suzy's product, then you do it. If Suzy doesn't pay you well enough, then you can promote someone else's product. You still *own* the list. You can change income streams, but you own the river.

Here is the affiliate manager's dirty little secret: Affiliate managers *know* that the opt-in e-mail list owners make the most sales, so they will often go and hunt down large opt-in e-mail publishers to be their affiliates. They even offer them special deals not available to the public. They will give them free products, offer higher commissions, make special offers to their customers, and so on. (I know this is true because I get these offers every day, since I have a large opt-in list.)

Your web site (the one you promote) should be telling people the benefits of joining your list. Then, after someone joins it, you can take them over to the lead product affiliate program. You could also use a pop-up that will pop up your lead product's affiliate page if someone decides to leave your site without signing up (so whether they sign up or not, they are still going to see this affiliate program's page on the way out).

I'm using the term *lead* product now because it is not your only product. It is the first product you show to potential customers. It is their first chance to buy from you. You only want to show potential customers one purchasing option at a time (so you don't confuse them). So pick a product that has a high sales rate and gives you a good amount of commission (you will usually want a low-cost product, since the first sale to a customer is the most difficult).

The purpose of this lead product is *not* to make a profit. I know that statement may be a little confusing for some people. That's right, you don't care if you make a profit on it or not. As a matter of fact, if you can just break even on it constantly, then you have an almost perfect Internet marketing system in place.

The only purpose of this first product offer is to try to break even on generating leads. For example, I advertise for $100 and get 100 leads to join my e-mail list. My first lead product makes two sales and earns me $100. I've now broken even. If I was an average affiliate, that would be a losing campaign. Since I'm now using the smart approach, I've only broken even but I'm ready to start dancing. I've just created 100 e-mail leads I can market to again and again—forever, for *free*. I can place more ads tomorrow and break even, producing another 100 free e-mail leads. I can roll out more advertising and start creating

1,000 free leads at a time. If I can continue to break even while selling a product to my list, then I'm on my way to success.

To earn a profit, all you have to do is sign up in another affiliate program and sell a second product to your list. If you want to earn more money, find a third affiliate program to promote. Sending out more e-mails to your list won't cost you any extra money!

There used to be a saying that he who has the gold makes the rules.

The Internet has changed that. Lots of companies with money can't earn a profit online. The new Internet marketing rule is, he who owns the list makes the rules!

■ UNDERSTANDING HOW TO BE LAZY

Most people have no idea how to be lazy when it comes to online business. I'm kind of lucky—being lazy comes pretty naturally to me. A lot of people won't follow the system I've just outlined to you, no matter how well it works. It doesn't matter if it is the best way to succeed as an affiliate (notice I didn't say it was the *only* way to make money—it's just the *best* way). They won't do it, because it sounds like too much work. I agree. At first glance it doesn't seem too easy.

The reason for this is that most people immediately think of an e-zine when it comes to creating an opt-in list. An e-zine is a newsletter that you send out daily, weekly, or twice a month by e-mail. It requires that you constantly be writing or coming up with new articles and information. You could also search out and publish other people's articles, but this also requires you to be constantly researching to find the best ones.

Notice that in the earlier sections I never said anything about running an e-zine. I said you were building an opt-in e-mail list. Some people will use an e-zine to do this. Others may just want to publish a free report by e-mail, or publish a free training series by e-mail.

This is accomplished by simply creating one free report, or by using one provided to you by an affiliate program of which you're a member (for example, I have a lot of free reports affiliates can use at http://www.bizpromo.com/free). You could also create a free report series using the system I teach in my report, "How to Create E-Mail Follow-Up." This is a much more lazy system than publishing your own e-zine. It requires you to create or find the free report series only one time, instead of being dedicated to publishing new articles constantly.

You write, find, or buy five articles to put up for your e-mail follow-up series. On each of these articles you keep selling your lead product and leading people to your affiliate web site. In other words, focus all of your beginning follow-up on just the *first* lead affiliate product you're selling. Keep hitting them with it. Provide good information so they read your series, but keep leading them back to the product page. Your goal, as mentioned before, is to generate enough sales for the first product you're an affiliate with to break even. If you can create breakeven within the first two weeks someone is a subscriber, then you can generate thousands of leads to profit from at *no* cost.

The goal is then to send out additional follow-ups and articles to your series whenever you get the chance. Send them every other week or every month. Find affiliate programs that sell related products or services. Sign up for them, then take any free articles they may provide you with and add them to your series.

This will enable you to be constantly earning multiple streams of income from the same e-mail leads. You only have to put the series up once. Then everyone who joins your list will be taken through every step in the series. Whenever you find another good affiliate program to promote, just add it on at the end. In time (at your leisure), your follow-up series may be 6 months, 12 months, or two years long. Every new subscriber goes through the series, and you profit every step along the way. You own the list. You make the rules.

"But I hate to write—and my affiliate program doesn't provide any free info to use." Let's say that is true. This excuse doesn't mean you have to be an online failure. If you choose not to write at all, then you can hire someone else to do it. Notice that I didn't say you *couldn't* write at all, because anyone can do it. You *choose* not to write at all. So hire someone else to write your free reports for you. Go to http://www.elance.com and post a project for "content." You'll find dozens of people ready and willing to write good articles for you—at a cost, of course.

■ TEN STEPS TO AFFILIATE SUCCESS

Let's break the entire system down into a simple step-by-step process you can follow—10 steps to setting up your own affiliate wealth funnel. Follow each step and watch the profits start coming in once you put your marketing in place.

➤ Step 1: Pick a Niche Market

Good marketers will always pick their customer base before they pick the product they want to sell. I've taught this to members time and time again. One of the most asked questions I get should never be asked at all: "I have this product—how do I sell it?"

The whole question is backwards. You are much better off asking, "Here are some prospects—what do they want to buy?" There is a world of difference between those two questions.

Always find your customers first. Then pick the product to sell to them. Once you know exactly who your customers will be, then you can make sure the product you're selling is what they've been looking for.

This strategy also gives you more opportunity for success. Let's say that you start building a list, but no one is buying the product you're selling. If your mind is focused solely on the product, then you have to give up and quit because no one is buying.

If you are customer focused, then you keep generating the leads, but you put a different product in the system. Since there are thousands of affiliate programs to sign up for, you can try all kinds of different products until you find the one your leads want to buy. Pick a niche market first—decide you will sell to real estate agents, paintball players, golfers, gardeners, or North Carolina residents. The potentials are unlimited. Find a group of people you can target online and go after them. The product is secondary in the decision process.

➤ Step 2: Find an Affiliate Program

Once you have a market you want to go after, then find an affiliate program to join. The purpose of this affiliate program is to help you break even while generating all your future e-mail leads. To accomplish this, the affiliate program must do the following:

➤ Pay good commissions. It will be hard to get yourself to the breakeven point if the first affiliate program you promote only pays 5 percent commissions (shoot for 25 percent or higher).

➤ Pay promptly. Most affiliate programs pay once a month for last month's sales. Try to avoid companies that only pay quarterly for your first program. It will be too long a wait for tangible rewards.

➤ Provide great value. This first product endorsement from you will determine how highly your customers think of you. Make sure it is an incredible value at a low cost.

Another desirable feature for this first program could be that they give you any free reports, free information, and so on, to use in promotions. The best-case scenario would be for them to provide the free report or the free series you need to be successful. You could just put their information on your autoresponder system. This will save you a ton of time and even money, if you were planning on paying someone else to do it.

Here are several places where you can research affiliate programs:

http://www.associateprograms.com

http://www.cashpile.com

http://www.2-tier.com

http://www.associate-it.com

http://www.i-revenue.net

http://www.referit.com

➤ Step 3: Buy a Domain Name

You will need your own domain name to be a successful affiliate, because your goal is to build *your* business, not the affiliate managers'. They send you checks, but you don't work for them. You work for yourself. You need to have your own domain name to build your own brand online. The place I use to both search for and purchase my domains is http://www.orderyourdomains.com.

Choose "Search Tools" at the top of their page and it will bring up several tools to help you create domain names you can use. Your goal is to create a domain name that is searched for online (they have a tool to help you do this) and that describes your business.

Look for short, easy to spell domain names. Finding a four-, five-, or even six-letter domain is virtually impossible now, but try to keep it short if you can. Don't go for words hard to spell or you'll lose out on a lot of potential visitors who hear about your page. They'll misspell your web address and miss your site entirely.

The rule for domain names is the same rule I follow for all marketing in general: Keep it simple.

➤ Step 4: Select a Web Host

You need your own web site for the same reasons you need your own domain name. You need to be building and branding your own business, not that of the affiliate manager. Sure, it will cost you some money, but you need to count this as a cost of doing business online.

I currently recommend ThirdSphereHosting.com as a fairly priced host under $25 a month. They have a very easy to use online management system and are quick to set up your account. You can even get your first month free (no commitment required) just for giving them a try. Try it out at http://www.bizpromo.com/freehost.html. There are other hosting possibilities as well. Bizminisites.com now offers hosting for simple mini sites for only $39.80 per year. That's cheap. Since you're not going to need a lot of pages starting out (your primary sales tool is the e-mail system, not the web site), this would be perfect for many affiliate businesses.

➤ Step 5: Set Up Your Autoresponder

This is the money machine of the affiliate system. You need a powerful autoresponder that follows up for you. There are a lot of autoresponder companies out there that come and go. I've dealt with a large number of them, but I definitely wouldn't recommend them all.

Below are the three systems I recommend. Each one has its advantages and disadvantages. Pick the one that's right for you and your plans.

1. Netofficetoolbox.com offers a 30-day free trial. You only need to the lowest-cost option.

2. BambooBizonline.com provides up to 50 autoresponders in one system.

3. Aweber.com gives you one autoresponder for $20 a month.

Once you've selected an autoresponder and have it set up, then it's time to upload your first free report series to it. You should use their login system and upload each of the letters. If you're running a five-day training series, set the autoresponder system to follow up on days 0, 1, 2, 3, and 4. This will send an issue to your subscribers every day.

When you upload your free reports, make sure to provide a link at both the top and bottom of the report to your affiliate sales page. Your goal is *not* to provide free information. Your goal is to make sales. The only reason you're giving away information is so that people will pay attention to your e-mails.

➤ Step 6: Design Mini Site Subscribe Pages

You only need two pages on your web site. Your front page will have a strong headline, some bullet benefits, and a subscribe form for the autoresponder you've chosen. The subscribe form itself is provided by whichever autoresponder company you joined in the previous step. You have to use the one they provide for best results.

The second page you need is a thank you page to thank people for subscribing to your e-mail series. You should make an endorsement here for your first lead affiliate product. A short endorsement should then end with a link to the affiliate sales letter on the affiliate manager's server.

➤ Step 7: Create a Pop-Up on Exit

While this step isn't absolutely essential, not following it will cost you money—sometimes a large amount of money. You want to install a pop-up box that appears when people try to exit your site. This should be a small box that has a two-paragraph endorsement for an affiliate product. Then it links to the affiliate program site. Insert this part of the code between the two head tags—it should be below the <head> tag and above the </head> tag:

```
<SCRIPT LANGUAGE="JavaScript">
var exit=true;
function leave() {
if (exit)
window.open('http://www.website.com/popup.html','',
'toolbar=no,menubar=no,scrollbars=yes,resizable=yes,
location=no,height=400,width=400');
}
// End -->
</SCRIPT>
```

When working with this code, fill in your own web address in place of "http://www.website.com/popup.html." For example, if the page you have uploaded to pop up on exit is http://www.netbreakthroughs .com/popup.html, then you need to fill that in there. Each of the other options can also be changed. You can change it to "menubar=yes" if you want people to see a menu bar. You can choose "scrollbars=no" if you don't want them to be able to scroll. You can also change the height and width of the pop-up by changing the "400" currently there to whatever size you need for your pop-up. The best way to size it correctly is to install the code and then test it by visiting and leaving your page.

Insert the following line anywhere in the web site below the </head> tag:

```
<BODY onUnload="leave()">
```

Once you've inserted these two codes, your pop-up on exit will now work. Whenever anyone leaves the page where you have the code installed, the pop-up will then occur.

➤ Step 8: Pick Your Second Affiliate Program

Go back to the affiliate directories and pick out a second affiliate program selling a product or service related to the first one. You will post this second affiliate program as another free report later on in your e-mail follow-up series.

This second program could be a higher-priced item, another item similar to the first one, or a residual income generator (like Netbreakthroughs). The keys to making the right choice are to make sure that it is for the same target market and that it relates to the first product somehow.

For example, if your first product is an e-book about Internet marketing, don't try to sell a set of golf clubs. Sell a membership for Internet marketing, web hosting, autoresponders, or something else that relates to the original subject. Build on the same idea.

Not all web sites work well for a first affiliate program. Netbreakthroughs' affiliate program is one of these. This may surprise you, but I don't recommend you use Netbreakthroughs as the first product you sell in your affiliate system. It doesn't produce enough up-front profit. It produces residual profits (long-term) so it makes a much better second or third recommendation to your list.

➤ Step 9: Set Up an Autoresponder

You're not going to advertise your second affiliate program. That would just divide up your attention and marketing budget. You are going to incorporate this affiliate program into your follow-up e-mail series.

Either create another free report or use one from the affiliate program, if they have one. Insert several links into the report to the affiliate program's web site. Now upload it to your autoresponder system. Schedule it 14 days after the last message. When someone subscribes to your e-mail series, they will now receive all five of your e-mail series selling the lead product. Two weeks later they will receive another free report from you for another affiliate product—with no extra work done by you.

Please note: You must always relate each e-mail from now on back to the original series the prospects signed up for. Remind them that they requested such-and-such a report, and tell them you have found this other report that provides them more information on the subject.

➤ Step 10: Repeat Steps 8 and 9

Keep repeating steps 8 and 9. Find more affiliate products and services. Use their free reports or create your own. Add them to the autoresponder system 14 days later than the last issue.

Everyone who subscribes to your series will get every follow-up message in the series. They will start at message 1 and then proceed through all of the messages. They will receive product offer 1 and then every affiliate offer after that. Your goal is to break even or better on the first affiliate program. Every e-mail they get from then on will be extra money in the bank for you.

The key to this system is that it doesn't require you to be involved at all. You aren't even sending out the messages! They are being sent automatically from an autoresponder. Set it up once and let it run forever. Whenever you notice another good product you'd like to add, just put it in later on in the system. It's that easy. It's the lazy affiliate marketing system. The next chapter will give you a step-by-step technique for pouring the most possible leads through your system.

42

The Lazy Person's Quick and Easy Guide to Affiliate Success—Part 2

Terry Dean

In the previous chapter I explained why most affiliates will fail, how to set up a profitable affiliate system, and the 10 steps to success as an affiliate. Now I'll give you the marketing techniques for the lazy affiliate. Having the right system in place won't do a thing for you if you don't generate traffic and leads.

First I'd like to emphasize the importance of focusing on your system. Far too many affiliates are in a rush to generate traffic, but it's just a waste of time and money to generate traffic too soon. If your system for generating leads and producing sales isn't in place, then your traffic doesn't matter. You need the Internet dynamic duo: system and traffic. They each have a part to play, and you need them both for maximum online profits.

■ HOW TO STAY LAZY AND STILL PROMOTE YOUR WEB SITE

There are quite a few techniques I *won't* be discussing here because they take too much time for the amount of money they generate for affiliates. Other techniques may work for certain kinds of businesses but are just too difficult for the average affiliate to pull off. Some techniques I wouldn't recommend for affiliates include:

➤ Free-for-all links pages

➤ Free classified ads

➤ Guaranteed traffic

➤ Publicity

➤ Banner advertising

➤ Opt-in e-mail marketing (except for e-zines)

➤ Postcards

The reason I wouldn't recommend free-for-all links pages or placing classified ads is simply that you'll have to work way too hard—and you'll produce minimal results at best. You could spend all month on those methods and only make a sale or two if you're lucky.

Guaranteed traffic simply doesn't work. I've tested it time and time again, and I have yet to find a bigger waste of money. I guess you could call spamming a bigger waste of money, but most experienced marketers won't fall for that garbage anymore. The guaranteed traffic promotions sell like crazy—but their originators are the only ones selling anything.

Publicity works extremely well for getting free traffic, but it really isn't open to most affiliates. Most reporters and interviewers would prefer to speak with the product owner or marketer rather than with an affiliate. Sure, there are a few publicity opportunities for affiliates, but they probably will require a lot of extra work and research.

Banner advertising simply costs too much for affiliates. As an affiliate you will only be getting a percentage of the sales price. This limits you in your ability to promote using banners since they have such a high cost and a low selling percentage. A product owner can promote using them, but they walk away with all the profits in their own sales.

You have to share your profits as an affiliate, so banner advertising usually isn't practical.

Ditto for e-mail marketing on services such as http://www .postmasterdirect.com. While e-zine ads can be placed at fairly low costs, using opt-in services like this are quite expensive. Since you're only getting a portion of the profits from each sale, you usually can't afford to use this method of advertising.

The sad thing is that postcard marketing and postcard decks will also probably fall into this category: too expensive for most affiliates. If you find a way to joint venture or co-op the postcards (having 3 to 10 partners on the card who pay for the mailing), then you can earn great profits. If you have to pay for the postcard yourself, you're probably out of luck when it comes to being an affiliate.

What follows are some of the techniques that you can use as an affiliate. I've divided them into two primary categories: free promotion and promotional methods that cost money. This will give a chance to both kinds of marketers.

Some affiliates don't have any money to spend on advertising. The free techniques are for them. Some affiliates have a little money, but don't have much time to spend. The paid techniques are for them. Sure, they'll cost you a few bucks, but they won't cost you the most important asset: time.

■ FIVE WAYS THE LAZY AFFILIATE CAN PROMOTE FOR FREE

Free promotional techniques are quickly disappearing, but there are still some working today. While I say these techniques are for the lazy affiliate, please understand they still require you to do something. The "something" you have to do just happens to be a whole lot easier than getting up early in the morning and going to work (or having to work a second job).

Don't fall for scams. There will be a multitude of voices pulling you this way and that telling you they have a free promotional technique that doesn't require any work. I've yet to find one that works. If you don't do at least a little work, then no work gets done. Most of the "quick and easy" methods you'll find out there drive traffic to the ones who came up with the idea, not to the thousands of people who sign up under them.

Don't jump on any of the "Brand New Incredible Overnight Traffic Building" bandwagons. There's a new one appearing every week—and they never work as well as the tried-and-true basic techniques. All they do is distract you from building an online business by making you think there's a big, secret traffic technique out there. There isn't. It isn't one trick that builds a business. It's the combination of doing several things right.

➤ Free Technique 1: Use Passive Marketing

I know you've been told to do a signature file before. Have you done it yet? Think about it for a moment. Hotmail.com built an entire empire, sold out to Microsoft, and did it all simply with a short signature file. They simply posted a short note at the bottom of everyone's e-mail about their service. While you won't be able to sign up millions of customers through a signature file, Hotmail has still proven they work. Every e-mail program gives you the ability to set up a signature file for yourself that goes out on every e-mail you send. Use it. Simply look in the instructions in your e-mail program for "Signatures."

While a signature file is a good passive marketing tool, it's not the only one. You could also have business cards made, highlighting your free report available by e-mail. Hand them out daily to people you come in contact with. Drop them into your bills when you pay them monthly.

Purchase a car sign to put on the side of your vehicle. Then, while you're sitting in traffic, your car is advertising your web site for you. You have the potential to create dozens of leads daily through this strategy.

➤ Free Technique 2: Free Article Submissions

Write short, 500-word articles and submit them to e-zines. E-zine publishers are always looking for good, valuable content to publish, and you're the one to give it to them. It's not nearly as difficult as you think!

Writing online is completely different from when you had to write reports in school. Sure, you need to use basic grammar. The difference is in the personality. When you write for online publishing, you simply write the same way you talk. English teachers will throw a fit over using the word *you* in writing, but *you* need to use *you* in online writing. Speak directly to your readers.

Forget that you're writing an article. Simply think of it as writing a set of instructions in a letter to a friend. This change in mind-set will allow you to open up and write more effectively for online publishing. Come up with a simple, step-by-step how-to article. Break up the 500 words you want to write into five different sections. Now just write 100 words about each step. This is no more than three paragraphs of writing, maximum, about each tip. It's easy.

The key is to start writing every week. You may not like what you see at first. Keep trying and keep writing. The tendency for most people is to simply give up and quit—at the same time giving up their dreams of being successful online.

Whether you ever write an article to submit or not, the Internet is still based on written communication. It's no accident that those who excel online are those who master this primary skill.

➤ Free Technique 3: Free E-Books

I love giving away free e-books for viral traffic. I have three that I've published and several I've published along with other authors. Put them together once and they drive traffic forever. You can see how I give them away on my main site at http://www.bizpromo.com. Not only do I give people permission to offer them free, but I also enable them to brand the e-books with their own links. This gives them an incentive to use my free e-books over those of everyone else I'm competing with. Not only do they get to give away valuable info, but they also get to generate repeat traffic back to their web sites.

The program I use for this is Wes Blaylock's ebookPaper. Simply create the pages of your e-book just as if you were creating a web site.

Link them all one to another and place them in the same directory. Then use the software to compile them into an e-book you can sell.

Not everyone who has tried to create an e-book has been able to turn it into a traffic virus like I have. The key to making it successful is to make it a very high-quality e-book. Ask yourself if the e-book is good enough to sell. If you can't sell it for $20, then it will never be passed around enough to turn into a real traffic virus.

➤ Free Technique 4: Articles to Lure the Search Engines

Use your articles to lure search engines into your site by posting them as free report pages. In other words, get maximum use from the articles you create. Use your articles in your autoresponders, to send to e-zine publishers, to create e-books, and to lure the search engines.

Subscribe to the free Wordspot report at http://www.wordspot.com. This regular report sent by e-mail will let you know the most popular search engine words and phrases. Once you know what people are looking for online, write about it.

Create 500-word articles about anything that relates to the products or services you're selling. Make sure the keyword phrase you're trying to get a good position on is used at least three times and no more than seven times in the article. Insert a title, keywords, and description in the meta tags. Link all of your articles to each other and to your main page. Then submit them to the search engines. You can use software such as Webposition Gold if you want to keep track of your positioning and to figure out how to modify your pages for best positions.

➤ Free Technique 5: Hang Out in Forums

I have several affiliates in Netbreakthroughs who earn a very good residual monthly income now simply by hanging out and participating in online forums. They basically visit forums every day or every other day and answer questions people are asking. You'll find that most forums don't have very many good, helpful people on them. So when you become one, people are automatically drawn to you. Simply post specific helpful answers and then include a link to your autoresponder or web site at the bottom of each message.

Don't advertise on forums. You are not there to advertise. You are there to network with other people in your niche. Never post just a link to your site. You can post a link at the bottom of your messages, but the readers should be able to learn something before they see your link. Then, once they get to the bottom where you've placed your link, they're ready to listen.

A great resource I've recently found to search multiple discussion boards at one time is http://www.messageking.com. Type in keywords and keyword phrases, and the Message King will find discussion boards where people are talking about that subject. You'll be able to collect discussion boards you will want to visit regularly, and you can also find new ones continually by doing regular searches. Every time you find an active discussion board on your topic, bookmark it. Then go back and visit it at least every few days for maximum effect.

■ THREE WAYS THE LAZY AFFILIATE CAN PROMOTE WITH MONEY

You have a little bit of cash and would prefer to spend some money instead of using your time online—or you refuse to write anything remotely resembling an article. Personally, I often prefer these methods, because it is much easier to roll out your advertising once you have proven your system works. If one e-zine works, then roll out to three. If those work, try ten. Keep expanding your advertising and you'll keep earning new profits.

➤ Money Technique 1: E-zine Advertising

When I'm first testing an offer or an autoresponder series, I like to go with e-zine advertising. If you can't earn money through advertising in e-zines, you'll find it extremely difficult to earn money any other way. E-zines out-pull every other marketing method in most cases. Although I've been able to earn money with classified ads and sponsor ads, my favorite type of advertising is solo ads. I will run one of the other types of advertising if solos aren't available for a particular e-zine. But if they offer solos, I'm going to run with them.

The best strategy for ezine advertising is to use the solo ad space to "sell" your free report (i.e., sell the readers on why they need the free report you have). Have them e-mail directly to an autoresponder system instead of visiting your web site.

You'll lose around 50 percent of your potential leads if you make them go to a web site to sign up for your autoresponder. Just promote the autoresponder directly from the ad. Don't even mention a web site at this point. Once they hit your autoresponder, you can use that to drive them to your affiliate sites.

➤ Money Technique 2: Co-Registration

Use co-registration services to build lists very quickly. In this method, one web site will run a contest and then have 5 to 20 e-zine publishers pay a deposit to be listed on the contest page. When people enter the contest, they also have the option of subscribing to any or all of the e-zines. The contest host then subtracts money (25 cents to $1 for each subscriber) from the deposit until your ad runs out. You get guaranteed subscribers.

This method builds lists very, very quickly, but it also has several major drawbacks. A big one is that these lists will not be as targeted as the ones you build on your own. These people are mainly interested in entering a contest. So the response rates and income you'll earn from this type of list will be lower than what you build on your own.

Here are some co-registration services you might want to check out:

http://www.zmedia.com

http://www.profitinfo.com

http://www.ezinecentral.com

http://www.myfree.com

http://www.funezines.com

http://www.internetfuel.com

http://www.bay9.com

➤ Money Technique 3: Pay-Per-Click Search Engines

You could create a large business by using the pay-per-click (PPC) search engines to build traffic quickly at very low cost. Use the Good Keywords software available free at http://www.goodkeywords.com to come up with hundreds of keywords for your web site.

Goto.com will make it very difficult to generate traffic as an affiliate. You can't drive traffic directly to an affiliate site—they don't allow it. If you send them to your free report page, they will probably reject the majority of your keywords.

For Goto.com, you need to combine free technique 4 with your autoresponder sign-up page. Simply post articles (they can be yours or other authors'), then put your e-mail subscribe at the bottom of each of these short pages. Use your keywords to drive traffic to the pages relating the article the keyword is about.

For the other PPC search engines, you won't have to be as sneaky. Simply come up with hundreds of keywords describing your free report (by autoresponder). Create a web page where people can subscribe to your autoresponder, by posting only a headline and bullet benefits. Upload the keywords to the PPC engines and start all your bids at one penny or less. You can up your bids once you've tested and proven your selling system to work.

Here are some of the other PPC sites:

http://www.7search.com

http://www.ah-ha.com

http://www.findwhat.com

http://www.kanoodle.com

http://www.sprinks.com

■ THE ULTIMATE WAY TO PROMOTE AFFILIATE PROGRAMS

This is a technique most people will never do, but it is my personal favorite way of generating free cash from affiliate programs. I receive well over a dozen affiliate checks each month, yet I rarely do anything to advertise any affiliate programs except my own.

My strategy simply uses affiliate programs as automatic streams of back-end income. Create an e-book you sell, and put affiliate links in it for resources. You could sell the e-book for a very low cost if you want ($17, for example). Your goal really isn't to make a profit on the sale of the e-book. You'd be very happy if you could break even while building a large e-mail list as you sell the e-book. Your goal with the e-book sales is to create long-term residual income in it through the affiliate links. Take some of Yanik Silver's recent projects as examples. He created *Autoresponder Magic* and *Million Dollar E-Mails* for this purpose. He sold them both below $20. Although he earned a very nice income when he first launched them (over $10,000 each), this wasn't his real goal. He sold them with full resell rights. This meant every one of the buyers had the ability to sell the product and keep all the money. This would definitely cut into his long-term sales. But his goal was to earn money from the affiliate programs highlighted throughout the e-book. Each of the sales letters (or autoresponder series) linked to an affiliate program where Yanik was a member. Yanik's affiliate checks started increasing monthly as more and more people were buying the product. The majority of buyers weren't even buying from him. They were buying from one of the resellers. He didn't care, though, because he still got affiliate checks no matter who sold the product.

You could almost compare this to the earlier free method of publishing a free e-book. The biggest difference is that buyers are much more likely to actually read through the e-book they purchased than they are to read the free one they were given. So, although the e-book doesn't get passed around as quickly as a free one, it actually has a higher readership rate.

After Yanik's breakthrough, numerous others have been copying this model and selling low-priced e-books with resell rights for the purpose of creating back-end affiliate commissions. *How to Create Killer Mini Sites* at http://www.bizpromo.com/minisites is an example of one of these types of products (they actually built a very lucrative pricing system into the model as well).

What about those who would want to take advantage of this model without writing or creating any products? If that describes you, then Tom Hau has created the program for you. He figured out this new marketing model and created the program at eBookwholesaler.com to provide a large number of low-cost e-books that you can sell and earn affiliate commissions on the back-end.

But the best-case scenario would be for you to create your own products. Either of the products I've just mentioned would put you in competition with thousands of others. If you create your own, then you really don't have any competition. You'll find that numerous people would love to own reprint rights to a well-written e-book and will pass it around for you—creating affiliate commissions for you all the way.

That's what I call being a lazy affiliate. Write an e-book once; put links in it; sell it; let others take over the job of selling it for you. And earn affiliate commissions every month from then on. That's the way I like to earn money.

43

How to Earn Maximum Profits from Affiliate Programs

Frank Garon and Terry Dean

The following excerpt was taken from a recent teleseminar tape set recorded by Frank Garon and Terry Dean. The series is called "Instant Internet Income Streams for Ordinary People." It teaches you how to build your own opt-in e-mail list and then develop multiple streams of income from it. This series is available in eight audio cassettes along with a complete transcript, phone consultation, and ad review at http://www.marketingcoachonline.com.

This excerpt focuses on generating affiliate income from your list and covers the major elements people miss when trying to make money from their lists. You have to follow the formula if you want huge sales in any affiliate program.

Terry: Frank, if I were to ask you to define an affiliate program for me, how would you do that?

Frank: Basically, an affiliate program is a product or service that you can represent. Some of them you can sign up for free. Some of them you have to pay to become a member. What happens is that you can recommend that product or service to other people and you'll get paid a percentage from the product or service that that particular company is offering. You'll get paid a commission check.

I can tell you, Terry, and the audience at home here today that affiliate programs can be very lucrative. I probably get between 15 and 20 different affiliate checks per month from different companies. So it's no small matter. It's very easy to make money via this fashion, but again, people, you do have to have legitimate products and services that make sense in the real world, if you expect to get paid and if you expect to make money.

Terry: I'd like to note the fact that there are affiliate programs for any type of product or service. It doesn't matter what type of market you're in. You could be selling to webmasters—there are affiliate programs that sell all kinds of products to webmasters, such as hosting, autoresponders training programs, things of that nature. You could be in the golf business—if you want to sell to golfers, there are affiliate programs that have golf clubs, there are affiliate programs for golf travel, there are affiliate programs for golf training.

In any niche market that you can pick out, there are going to be affiliate programs out there that sell this market—programs that you can sign up in, and most of the time you can sign up in them for free. I recommend that you always test out the product. Always test the product before you sell it. But still, the affiliate programs are actually free. You don't have to pay a fee for distributorship for affiliate programs, in most cases. But you can sign up for them and you can start to promote their products.

Some directories that you can start to look up are at:

http://www.associatesprograms.com

http://www.cashpile.com

http://www.cj.com

These three directories are places where you can do a search for any niche market and find affiliate programs relating to that market. Now again, these affiliate programs are usually free, but we almost always recommend that you buy the product first. We're not saying that you have to buy every product a company sells, but buy at least one product from that company before you ever affiliate with it.

Don't you agree, Frank?

■ DON'T SELL ANYTHING YOU DON'T OWN YOURSELF

Frank: Well, I'm glad to hear you say that and I hope everybody listening to this takes that at face value, because one of the gripes that I have about Internet marketing is the fact that some people (and certainly they should know better) will just sell anything to anybody, at any time, without ever owning it or doing a real hard evaluation of it first.

And yes, the only stuff I recommend is stuff that I own. Either I have physically purchased it, or I have had, in a couple of instances, a courtesy copy sent to me for review. Only if and when I'm satisfied that it will help me in my own business will I then recommend it to other people. We've talked about credibility before and how important it is. It's the same thing here. If you're going to represent pixie dust and garbage to people and hold it out to be something of value just so that you can make a commission check, it's only going to backfire on you. It's not worth it.

You have one reputation, you have one chance to earn people's trust. Therefore it's very important that you represent products and services that you honestly believe in. And again, people make mistakes. Hey, I backed one or two horses that didn't make the race, but I had always done my homework, I had always invested my own money, and I had always felt confident in them. Even if, God forbid, something didn't work out, people weren't mad at me. They knew I was credible, they knew I had done my homework.

And again, you just can't go to a sheet of affiliate programs and pick them at random. They have to be coherent, they have to tie into your web site, they have to tie into what you are trying to represent. And with the amount of affiliate programs that are out there for any different product or service you could ever imagine, the average person should have no problem finding legitimate and credible products and services to represent.

Terry: Well, I definitely agree. Reputation is everything online. One phrase that I always like to use while I'm teaching people about online marketing is that "Money comes and money goes, but your reputation lasts forever." Everything that you sell in your business, everything that you do in your business should work on building your reputation. Never go through and destroy it for a quick profit. A lot of people are quite willing to do that, just for a big profit. One day they represent a product that they know isn't that great, just because they can earn a lot of money. We're telling you never to do that, because the Internet is about long-term income. We're not telling you to get rich quick on the Internet. You notice we never called this set "Get Rich Quick Online."

What we're telling you is that any ordinary person, *anyone* can build a business online. Both Frank and I are very ordinary people. Frank was a truck driver from New Jersey and I was a pizza deliverer in Indiana. And if we can do it, you can do it too. But the key to this is that it's a business. You have to build your reputation, and your business will live or die on its reputation. Always make sure that any affiliate product that you sell has good value.

Besides having good value and really helping your customer, what other types of things do you look for in the affiliate programs, Frank?

■ BUILD MULTIPLE STREAMS OF INCOME TO THE SAME CUSTOMER BASE

Frank: Well again, Terry, things that make sense. Things that fit into my marketplace that I've developed already, things that my opt-in readers and my web site visitors would need. You know I'm an Internet marketer, I'm a network marketer, so I tend to stick to those products and services.

I'll recommend traffic resources, places to advertise, places to get newsletter subscribers, places to learn how to optimize your web site for search engines, places to get pre-qualified leads for your network marketing program or your affiliate program. It's all congruent and it's all tied in.

Recently I branched out, in a sense, but in another sense I didn't branch out. What I started to do was actually represent some personal growth material and some financial planning or debt management software. The reason that I do that now is because, in my opinion, anybody who's trying to make money from home, you need to have self-discipline, number one; you need to have confidence; you need to have good business sense. And again, that's why we keep recommending things like *Think and Grow Rich* and *Scientific Advertising.*

But at the same time, you know you're running a business here. You have to be the CEO of your own company, and that does include money management. So although I specialize in Internet marketing and network marketing, I've also recently added in these couple of other personal growth and financial management products—you know, *Think and Grow Rich, Rich Dad, Poor Dad,* those types of books.

The reason I do that is because it's congruent with what I'm teaching people. You're not going to see an ad for aluminum siding in my web site; you're not going to see an ad for Time Sharers for Aruba in my newsletter. It's not congruent with what I offer to my readers and what I'm known for. But even if all you sold was fishing supplies or embroidery material, there are so many different things, and so many different products and services that you can recommend. You really do not have to limit yourself just to Internet marketing. It just turns out that's my specialty—that's what I fell into.

One of my hobbies is trains, both model and layouts and real trains in real life. I know for a fact that I could make full-time income just by finding various affiliate programs and various products and services that I could represent in an area that I'm really passionate about, one that really interests me as a hobby. Internet marketing and network marketing are great, but at the same time do not overlook your hobbies. I think sometimes hobbies might even be easier for people to get started in and easier for people to get excited about.

■ FOLLOW YOUR PASSION AND YOU'LL FIND YOUR PROFITS

Terry: One thing I like to tell the people I consult with is that it's much easier to run a business if you're passionate about the subject. If you hate the subject then you're always going to find it difficult to run a business. And one of the old statements that people make in business is that you should always try to pick a business that you would do even if you weren't getting paid for it. Well, that wouldn't quite work for me, because I don't think I would do anything if I weren't getting paid for it! But it does give a real principle here, and that is, if you can find your passion, you'll be able to find your profits. And this goes for any type of business.

Although my specific products are in the Internet marketing field, I've consulted with a lot of clients all across the board, in every kind of site that you can think of. And the same tools that we talk about for Internet marketing, the same type of systems that we talk about for network marketing, and the same type of system that we talk about for information marketing, work in all these different businesses.

For example, one of the web sites that I've worked with was the Wedding Products web site. They sold wedding products and we were able to generate over twenty thousand hits in a week to them. We were able to basically build their ground and build their list in just over a week or two. Because guess what? That was what their passion was, that's what they wanted to sell, it's what they knew about.

So what I want to tell people here is you find your passion and you'll find your profit. One of the people that I consulted with before had a web site that sold health products and cigarettes. Imagine how those two themes seem together. They were selling health products and cigarettes on the same web site. That didn't make any logical sense whatsoever! So although we say you can sell anything, find your passion, and make sure that if you have a web site, everything on that web site is following the same theme.

A golf product web site should only be selling things that involve golf or have to do with golf. If you have a web site about Internet marketing, that web site should only be about Internet marketing. It shouldn't be about health products also. Try to keep following one subject, one theme, so you don't confuse your visitors.

I'd like for us to talk about how to market the program to our list. We've already talked about the importance of building our list. Now we're going to represent this product to our list. Exactly how do we want to sell it to our list? Do we just want to place the ad given to us by the affiliate program in our list? Or do we want to do something else?

■ HOW TO BRAND YOURSELF

Frank: It's strange that you asked me that, Terry, because that's something that I'm passionate about, and I want to get this point across to everybody at home. We've talked so far about building an opt-in list, the importance of building a newsletter, and again the thing that I see people doing is they want to get 400 subscribers together really fast, whether they buy them for World Wide List or do ad slots or whatever.

They want to get 400 strangers on a list, they want to use the same ads that every other affiliate representing their product or service uses, and then they want those 400 strangers that maybe have only been reading them for three weeks to go buy a ton of products or services from them—and it doesn't work like that.

What you need to do is build rapport with your readership first. There's a right way and a wrong way to do things, and you can argue with me all day, but all I'm saying is, this is the right way because myself, Terry, and everybody else's paychecks that I know are doing good, all do things in a very similar fashion.

You have to brand yourself. You have to build rapport with people. You have to give people a reason to know, like, and trust you. You have to give people a reason why, out of everybody on the Internet that they could spend their money with, why they should go to you.

And that's a mistake that most people make: They don't do that first. They want the money first, and they say, "Well, I have numbers on my list, but I'm not selling." And I look at their newsletter and see that they're not talking to them like human beings, they're just running a gigantic classified ad. Nobody wants that. That's not a way to get through to people.

So what you have to do again—and you don't have to be the world's greatest speaker, you don't have to be a poet or an elder statesman, you don't have to be Winston Churchill, you don't have to be me. But what you do have to be is yourself, and you have to be able to talk to people and communicate to them the value of what you're recommending to them and why it would help them.

I will repeat that: the value of what you're offering them and why it would help them. From the value end of it, you add value by telling your readers, "I bought this product. This thing is great—it grew hair on my head and I'm two inches taller. It's just wonderful go-juice. You've got to have this stuff. You're going to dance a jig, you're going to be younger, you can stay up twenty-five hours a day. That's why I like this stuff, that's why I want you to try it, because I love you and I want you to be happy."

How much better is that, how much more productive you're going to be doing that than just running an ad: "Acme Moon Juice, it's the greatest, buy some (Click Here)," and your links say "moon juice.com/associates/cgi/number two million ten." There's no relationship there, there's no rapport there. And it's easy, it's so easy to build rapport, just by being an average decent human being who might have an opinion or two. It's so easy to do that, that I say you are being criminally negligible to your business if you just run generic ads to your list. You're just costing yourself money.

■ DON'T SELL—PRE-SELL THROUGH REVIEWS

Terry: I would like to mention that one of the really powerful features when you have your own list is, if you send out the ad, make it personal by saying what you yourself got out of the product. Don't just use the ad that's provided.

I'll call this the review method. I tell my prospects the good features of a product, and I'll even tell them something about the product that I didn't like. If it's like a product that's shipped to me, I might tell them that I learned these three things from the product, but the product was ugly, or whatever else. I didn't like how it looked.

The power in this is now you are believable. There is so much hype online, there's so much garbage, there are so many lies—we might as well come out and call it what it is: lies online. People don't believe anything you say anymore.

So what you've got to do is, anytime you want people to listen to you, or whenever you want people to take action, you have to do something to build your credibility. The first thing that you do to build your credibility is you're going to actually provide them information to your list. You're going to be showing your personality, showing who you are to your list. The second thing that you can do to specifi-cally build credibility in the product that you are selling is not to make it sound like the most wonderful thing in the world, but to tell good parts about it and even reveal one negative part about it.

For example, recently Jim Daniels, who runs a large newsletter, published a quick notice about my membership site over at Netbreak-throughs. Within 24 hours he signed up an average 135 people for his endorsement of my site. But guess what? He started the whole en-dorsement with what he didn't like about the web site, which was the fact that I reviewed his newsletter and the ads results weren't very good. So he first said that he didn't like that part, but he started re-viewing the site even more, and he said he found all these good parts to it, so he recommended it to his readers.

And with just that simple endorsement—remember, it was free for him to send it out to his list—he signed up over 130 people to a mem-bership site that pays him every month. So he's created for himself a monthly income from now on, through one letter to his list, and basi-cally it was just his straight opinion of what the site was about. And he started out with a bad part!

Frank: Hey, Terry, I need you to do me one favor. If you ever review my products or services, just be gentle because I'm very sensitive. I need you to do that for me. But all kidding aside, that is a very valid point.

One thing that I want to mention is, in my newsletter or even on my web site, in most cases I do not give the standard company pitch. It's absolutely imperative that I make the first paragraph say why I like what I'm recommending. The company's standard letter might be excellent copy, written by a professional copywriter, proven guaran-teed results, and so on. And they may be telling me it's the greatest thing, and that if I run it to my list I'm going to make a million bucks.

You know what? I don't care, I'm still going to put a paragraph or two after the top with my own advice and my own reasons why *I* rec-ommend the product. I even do that sometimes in the articles I run in my newsletter. You want to develop people's trust in you, you want people to listen to you and buy from you.

I look at it this way: If all you're doing is running the same ad that the rest of the world is, there's nothing making you stand out as num-ber one—or even number two, if you run the same ad in the same way as everybody else. Guess what? You didn't brand yourself.

■ BRAND YOURSELF WITH INTEGRITY

You have to brand yourself. I want people to say, "I don't make a move without Frank. I don't buy anything until Frank tells me to. I want to know what Frank thinks before I spend a dime on anything." And do you know what? I have that trust, and I say this in a humble, respectful way, certainly not in a vain way. And the people listening to this conversation, I hope, get what I'm telling you here because this is the key to your making money.

We talk about being honest and up-front; we talk about being respectful to your readers; we talk about only representing good products and services. We keep talking about branding yourself, making them come back to you. That is the key to my income here. It's not because I know search engines. I just hit Webgoldposition, and whatever it does, it does—that's my search engine strategy. It's not perfect, and I don't have all the answers to anything. But I do know one thing and that is, by branding myself and by getting people to come back to me and my site, eventually it is not that hard to develop a loyal following and actually be able to influence the buying decisions of tens of thousands of people.

I know that I can run anything to my list, any legitimate product or service that is relevant to what I'm about, and I will make money because my readers have that trust in me. I'm not saying that I bat a thousand every time, but for publishing for almost three years now, I have developed a loyal enough following that it has secured my income. People expect that when they buy something from me, it's going to be good. And that's the key to the Emerald City right there.

Just be credible, brand yourself. Then, if you write your own opinion—and again, you don't have to be eloquent, you don't have to be grammatically perfect, you don't have to make every sentence hypnotic writing. Try simply being yourself for a change. So many people on the Internet write in a way that sounds automated—boring stuff. Why don't you say something different, say what you think, say what you feel. I think people will buy from you just out of loyalty if nothing else.

Terry: In this last set of comments, you've said a lot about branding and about loyalty. These are words that big companies are desperately chasing after. They're seeking ways to develop a brand online; they're seeking to create a loyalty program where customers come back to them. But what I want our listeners to see here is that we brand ourselves in one major way, and we do that basically by building our list and then, in whatever we put out to them, having integrity in front of our list constantly.

By *integrity* I mean staying honest, only representing good products, showing our personality. I include all of that in this one word when I say "integrity in front of our list." That's how we build our brand, and that's how we build the loyalty program. That's what all these multimillion-dollar corporations are seeking, but they haven't found the secret. You now have the secret that they're losing millions of dollars trying to find.

■ MULTIMILLION-DOLLAR LOYALTY FOR FREE

Frank: And the great thing is that we do it for free. I spend exactly zero dollars a month on advertising. I've done all this for free. I'm not saying my way is the right way, the only way, the perfect way. But when I started this, I did not have a lot of money. But I had a brain, a mouth, and two hands, and it got me to this point.

We present a business model on this series of tapes and in this seminar, and anybody can take the information and duplicate exactly what we're doing. But when I started on the Internet, you still had to pay to buy Internet browsers. These marketing courses, these e-books and the search engine tools—none of this was around back then. None of these places where you can go and pay for subscribers were around. None of what Terry and I do right now was available when we started out.

People starting in this business now can take advantage of things that we didn't have. A person coming into it today can do it faster and easier than I did. I had to do a lot of learning and improvising; nowadays they drop the tools in your lap. But what you need is a little bit of money. Buy a couple of good courses, do a little bit of experimenting, and put together a decent web site and a list, and you're off and running.

Terry: I hope people really listen to what we're saying about this system. Don't argue with us, don't debate about what we are handing you, because it took us years to learn this. It took me a long time to learn that any ad that I sent out to my list needed to have a little bit of my personality added to the top. I've sent endorsed offers to my list for free, and made $34,000 or more from one offer.

But guess what? I've also tried it the other way, which is just to use the ad copy given to me by someone else and send it to the same list, and received no orders. Do the math—which one would you rather have, the $34,000 or the zero? And I'm talking about a big list—my list now is 60,000 subscribers, but if I publish someone else's ad there are still times when I don't get any response. People who know me are waiting for my acknowledgment, they're waiting for my opinion, they're waiting for me to put my seal of approval on something before they'll sign up and join it, because of the branding message that we're talking about.

■ OTHER TYPES OF E-MAIL FOLLOW-UP

Terry: Frank, do you use other types of e-mail follow-up besides your main list?

Frank: You mean to get my product or service out in front of people's eyes?

Terry: Yes.

Frank: I really like to use autoresponders. One of the other things I look at when I'm evaluating a potential affiliate program is not only what kind of sales letters they have that I can add my two cents to, but also what kind of autoresponder letters they have. Do they have little e-books or a little download that will give people a teaser, a sample of what this is all about?

When I say "Free report tells you seven ways to get more traffic to your web site—click here," what will happen is they'll go to one of my autoresponders that's coded with my affiliate link. They'll get a listing of a series of free reports, and at the end of every report there's a call to action: "If you like what you see, click here now."

To me, that is the greatest thing since sliced bread, because even as good as my newsletter is, it's not perfect—I'm not going to turn anybody on to what I'm offering the very first time I put it out to them. People need five to seven contacts before they're going to buy. And even with a very loyal list like I have, I can scrape some money off the top. I can make some money just by putting something out there. But boy, if I get them into an autoresponder, look out.

It's the same thing with e-books. These little e-books are so great. You give somebody a good bit of information, you give them a free sample, so it's not just a sales pitch but it's good, relevant information. You didn't have to write the e-book, you didn't have to compile it, you don't have to do anything except to make sure it goes to your link, and that's it.

So these are the other tools that I like to use. And I use my list. If you took everything else away from me, my list makes me my money.

So don't overlook autoresponders. Your goals should always be to get people into a list, an autoresponder, a free report, something that's going to woo them a little bit, and eventually they're going to see something of value. They're either going to buy it or they're going to unsubscribe.

If you give people a free report or a free e-book, they think, "I realize this isn't the full version, and I'm skeptical of buying stuff and I only have limited ad dollars. But here's this guy who gave me a very good free sample of what he has to offer. I'm going to plunk down the $50 or $100, $500, because he gave me a nice little preview of what it's all about." So those three strategies—loyal newsletter list where you're giving a personal view, autoresponders, and e-books—are the three things I use the most.

■ WHAT'S THE BIG SECRET TO SELLING AFFILIATE PRODUCTS?

Terry: We're going one further and that is, when you're in an affiliate program, by its nature you have thousands of competitors who are all selling the same affiliate program. Of course, loyalty from your readers matters to you. But how do you make the product even better for your customers than what the other affiliates are offering? Do you offer an extra bonus or anything else? And if so, what kinds of bonuses do you add to the offer?

Frank: Here's my super secret that I wasn't prepared to reveal, but Terry, you're holding my feet in the fire here. What I do is give freebies. Not only do I review it and write a personal note, and not only do I say to them, "Hey, I bought this and I think it's good and here's why," but I will also make an offer at the end. Maybe it's "Buy this and I'll give you five free ads in my newsletter." And I don't use paid advertising in my newsletter, so this has high perceived value. Or I might say, "Buy this and I will give you another product or service that I have full reseller rights to." Or I would say, "Buy this and you can get on the phone with me free for 30 minutes, and ask me whatever you want." These days I get paid $100 an hour to consult with people, so a half hour is actually a $50 value, not a made-up number.

By doing these things, I now make the product attractive. I even have offers where I can give somebody a free two-night and three-day vacation in a hotel. All they have to do is pay $5 to redeem the thing and they can have a free vacation on Uncle Frankie in Las Vegas or Cancun.

There are many different ways and different techniques that you can enhance whatever you're selling. But you don't want to make it ridiculous—you don't want to say, "Buy my e-book and I'll give you a free Rolls-Royce." That's just silly.

But what you can do is add so many extras and benefits and freebies that people are going to say, "You know what, even if this thing turns out to be junk for some odd reason, the freebies that he's giving me here are more than worth the purchase price." You have to do anything you can to break down the buying resistance and earn people's trust.

■ YOU DON'T HAVE TO BE THE BEST— JUST BE DIFFERENT

You don't even have to be perfect. I can tell you, I'm not the world's best ad writer, the world's best copywriter, or the world's best offer maker, but I'm always out there and I'm not afraid to get crazy.

In my newsletter sometimes I'll run an "Uncle Frankie's crazy special," why I want to give you $1,000 worth of stuff with every $50 purchase. And then I'll make a case. I'll say, "Look, this isn't just some number I'm making up. Here's the actual value of what I'm going to give you, and here's the reason why I do it. Maybe today I got bit by a rabid bat and I'm completely insane, and I'm just writing my newsletter and I don't even know what I'm doing, but take advantage of me. " Or, "Hey, my daughter graduated from junior high and I'm in a good mood. Catch me before I go back to my usual grouchy self. Buy today." I do anything I can do, any kind of offer, anything I can do to get people's attention.

I'm going to give you another secret to success. I'm revealing for the first time the two secrets that make me the most of my money. The second secret is that part of this is just show biz. And when I say *show biz* I don't mean it in a negative way—I don't mean phony or contrived. But you're competing with a crowded marketplace. Some of these programs have thousands of people in them. You've got to do anything you can to draw attention and response.

So if I act a little goofy once in a while and that's what works for me, great. Or if I say something deliberately controversial, great—it gets people's attention. Some people might write eloquently; others might write incredibly well from a standpoint of "Hey, I'm an expert, this is my specialty. Let me tell you in a little more detail why this particular offer is good for you." There are a lot of different ways to do it, but essentially this is show business. *Show* your people why they should buy from you.

There is a certain guru out there, and I don't trust 99 percent of what he says, but there's one thing he told me that has put a ton of money in my pocket. He told me years ago that you have to have unlimited resources on the Internet. Don't be afraid to give them out.

If you want to make an offer today and put $500 in your pocket by tonight, sell some ad space. Put a link on your web site, give them a free e-book, get on the telephone with them, give them some free advice, write them a free report that is exclusively for people who purchase that product in that time frame. Give them a free vacation, buy them dinner, do whatever you have to do.

■ THERE'S A LOT OF NOISE OUT THERE

You have many different options to make yourself stand out in the crowd, but it is a crowded marketplace and you have a lot of noise to overcome, and a lot of reluctance.

Many sellers out there are saying, "My product is great, it's top dollar, and it's featureless. Buy it, buy it, buy it." That's who you're competing against. You're competing with other people who are obscuring your message. They're helping to gum up the works.

A legitimate buyer who is in need of your product or service has to go through so much noise just to hear your message, that you have to do anything you can to make it easier for them.

In my experience, by being consistent and outspoken, by being willing to make an offer, by being willing to pile on so many goodies that a person can't resist, and by only recommending products and services that I could honestly recommend to my mother, I have been able to achieve great success in this business. A guy who drove a tractor trailer for a living for 15 years, or someone who went bankrupt trying to make money working from home, could figure out how to do this and turn it into a six-figure income. Anybody listening to this conversation could do this. I am no brain surgeon—and if you knew me or were paying to see me speak in person, you would say the same thing—but I do know how to make money.

So I hope everybody's taking the advice that Terry and I are giving you on these tapes and it's really hitting home, because this isn't theory. This is what we do to put money in our pockets and food on our family's table every day of the week, every week, all year long.

Terry: The reason I asked Frank Garon to reveal that to you is that it's so important to know how to make an offer. It's the direct marketing principle that works in any business. If you can make an offer, make it irresistible. Add in extra bonuses that are worth as much as or more than what someone is buying, and then tell people why you're doing it.

You always have to have a reason why. There's an old marketing phrase: "Tell me why and then I'll buy." Tell people why you're doing it. It's your birthday, it's your wife's birthday, or whatever the special is. The product might not be done yet and you're selling it right before it's done, so buyers will get a discount. There are all kinds of possible reasons. Have a discount, have an offer, have specials to add on, and then tell them why, and you'll create an incredible amount of sales in any product, in any market, with any offer you make to your list.

■ WHAT TO DO IF YOU OWN THE AFFILIATE PROGRAM

Now I want to change directions and talk about the other viewpoint. So far we've been talking about being an affiliate and how to make money as an affiliate. I want to spend a few moments on being an affiliate manager, being the owner of the affiliate program, and how you can use this to earn the most money.

I've run several affiliate programs, which means that I've had thousands of people out there selling my products. One of the things people don't tell you before you get an affiliate program is the fact that about 95 percent or more of the affiliates you sign up aren't going to do anything. They're going to earn no money. All they're going to do is e-mail you and ask why they don't have any sales. If you check their traffic you'll find they have one or two hits, and those were from their own visits to see why they didn't have any sales.

The people who are important, the people you're going to be looking for to sign up in your affiliate program, are going to be people who are e-zine publishers. Is that any surprise? Is it any surprise that you're looking for people with large opt-in lists to be an affiliate?

So when you run an affiliate program, you're going to look for e-zine publishers to affiliate with you, and you're going to make an opt-in offer they can't refuse, in the same way we've just been talking about making offers people can't refuse. You'll offer them higher commissions, and you'll offer them free products.

There are several big companies online whose whole marketing strategy is based on going to e-zine publishers and giving them free copies of every product they create, and then giving them a little bit higher commission than the average affiliate. That's because they earn their money from those people who are making endorsements to their lists. They know this, and they tap into it. So it doesn't have to take years to build a list. If you have a product that's selling, that people are going to want to buy, you become the affiliate manager, go to the people who spent years developing their lists, get them to make an offer to their lists, and you split the profits.

The program I recommend when you're starting your own affiliate program, if you're selling any type of e-books or visual downloads, is ClickBank, available at http://www.clickbank.com. They'll actually handle the affiliates for you. They'll handle the tracking for you, and they'll even pay the affiliates for you so you don't have to keep track of that. So if you are selling digital downloads, they're a great one to start with for your first affiliate program. If you're selling other types of products and you need a shopping cart or something of that nature, I suggest you go to http://www.netofficetoolbox.com. It has an affiliate program built in with shopping carts, autoresponders, and things of that nature. It will help you to set up your own affiliate program to sell your products. To set up a basic affiliate program simply requires that you get an affiliate software company to run it for you and then go out and start finding big publishers. Start finding people who have lists and get them to promote your product.

Notice that I didn't tell you to set up an affiliate program and just put a link on your site for people to sign up for it. That's the slowest way in the world to sign up good affiliates. The best way to sign up good affiliates is go to them. Send them e-mails, send them free samples of what you're selling, contact them, make them an offer they can't refuse.

If someone contacts you, Frank, as an affiliate, what kinds of offers do you get to make you stand up and take notice?

■ WHAT IS THE NUMBER ONE THING THAT ATTRACTS A SUPER-AFFILIATE?

Frank: Well, I could say it's got to be a good product. I sell things that I get peanuts on, that are barely worth my selling them, from a

business standpoint, but I represent them and recommend them because they are good for my readers. I'd love to make 99 percent of
the sale, and I'd like it to be a $200 item that will get my attention.
But what I look for is a good product or service that makes a difference in my readers' lives and in my web site visitors' lives. If I make
$2.00 here or $200 there, I don't care, but it's got to be a good product or service. It has to be professional, it has to have no typos, and
it has to be something unique.

I get pitched on probably two to five deals a week: "Hey Frank, I
know you've got a big newsletter. I want to give you a free sample and
then would you please send it out to your list? And we'll pay you a
nice commission and stuff." I could just be a sellout and continually
recommend new stuff, but not everything that everybody puts together is really worth selling.

Probably a quarter of my product line consists of about five tools
that I think the average person cannot be without. So I continually recommend those. Then there are another five or ten that I'll rotate—I'll
recommend one this month, and then I won't talk about it for a month.
I'll rotate it out and bring in probably one new product a month—one
good product or service each month.

I know people who consistently have good products, so anytime
they come out with another one they automatically get a review and a
recommendation from me. This is the case anytime Terry, Lee Benson,
or Marlon Sanders comes out with something. With people like that, I
get excited when they come out with a new product. And honestly, I'd
rather that keep happening than having to find new people to sell or
promote new products.

If you can build readers' trust, they'll listen when you say, "Hey,
why not get the entire volume of Frank Garon's products?" or why not
get the entire volume of Terry Dean, Jimmy Brown, or whoever. When
you build loyalty and trust, you can easily sell several products or services from the same creator.

I'm very welcoming and I am very willing to consider anybody's
affiliate offer. I tell people to send it to me, and if I think it's good,
they're going to make some good money because I'm going to recommend it to my list. But at the same time, I have to tell you I am very,
very picky and only the best of the best sees the light of day. On my

web site and in my newsletter I'm very protective of my readers and I'm very, very, cautious of what I recommend to them.

Frank Garon is an ex-truck driver who went from making $14.25 an hour to earning more than $130,000 a year solely from affiliate programs. Find out how Frank can help you change your financial future at www .InternetCashPlanet.com.

44

Confessions of a Radical Super-Affiliate

Jason Mangrum

As you read this chapter, you will discover several key elements of becoming a radical super-affiliate. I'll start by telling you that almost every manual, course, or book you have ever read about affiliate marketing is *wrong*. Why? Simply because most of them only focus on signing up for several different free affiliate programs, and using them to create your success as an affiliate.

What they *don't* tell you is that most of these pre-made, free affiliate programs have been out for who knows how long and already have hundreds or even thousands of affiliates promoting their products and services, just like you are. This means that you have more competitors for the same product or service than you can imagine.

Now, this isn't necessarily a problem, as super-affiliates know the proper steps to take in order to still generate commissions from these saturated programs. However, I will show you a little secret that you can use to not only start at the top of any product or service you choose, but to be possibly the *only* radical super-affiliate selling for your chosen company! Just imagine how powerful this secret would be in the right hands—*your* hands.

By the time you have completed this chapter, you will have learned at least four things:

1. The secret no one else is telling you about radical super-affiliates.

2. A simple formula for creating radical super-affiliate success.

3. How you can virtually take control of any company or business you choose, immediately be thanked for it, and become a well-respected authority figure in that company at the same time.

4. How three words and a simple request positioned me as a point of authority in the minds of every reader of this book (including you).

Ready? Let's get started.

■ THE SECRET NO ONE ELSE IS TELLING YOU ABOUT RADICAL SUPER-AFFILIATES

You are about to learn a powerful secret that could change the way you do affiliate marketing forever. Here's part of it: Most affiliate programs don't work. Yes, it's sad, but true. The fact is that more than 95 percent of all affiliates never make a dime on anything they promote. From the minute they sign up, they are put in direct competition with anyone and everyone who is an affiliate of the same company.

I want you to imagine for a minute that you have been employed by a direct door-to-door type business. Let's call it Jason's Business Monthly. Imagine you have been put in charge of selling magazines for this company, and that you will receive a nice commission for every subscription you sell, going door-to-door. This company has been around for a while and has established a good name in the community. They also provide a well-known and appreciated service, so you should have no problem with selling these magazines like crazy. Right?

Wrong. The truth is, more than likely nearly every house in that community has already been presented with this same offer, simply because the company *has* been around for a while and has no doubt already sold a large percentage of magazines in the first few years of establishment. Most of their sales are now coming from current customers who pay a monthly fee for the service. You could, of course, possibly make a few new sales from people who have just moved in, or from people who passed on the offer the first time around, but that certainly isn't going to make you the kind of money you desire.

By now, I can almost hear you saying, "Okay, I understand your analogy, but couldn't I just find a new company that hasn't been around very long, become an affiliate, and sell their products and services like crazy?"

Yes, you *could* do that, but again, I wouldn't expect a huge commission check every month from them either. The reason is that such companies are brand new and have yet to become well-known and respected throughout the Internet community. So, once again, fewer sales.

At this point, you're probably thinking, "Well, there probably isn't a way to make a lot of money through affiliate programs then, is there?" Actually, no—unless you're already a super-affiliate. Not for the most part, anyway, and not with regular affiliate programs.

So this chapter is going to deal with the subject of affiliate marketing in a slightly different manner than any other book, course, or manual out there. I'm talking about radical super-affiliates.

I deliberately place the word *radical* in front of *super-affiliate* when speaking about my new approach to affiliate marketing. Part of the reason I do this has to do with positioning, which you will learn about in this chapter, but another part has to do with the fact that it is a secret twist on affiliate marketing in general.

Imagine once again that you are working for Jason's Business Monthly, selling magazines door-to-door. Suddenly you begin to realize that you will never make the kind of money you want just from selling these magazines. So do you quit selling magazines for Jason's Business Monthly? No. You decide to get smart about it and do some much-needed research on the company, and you discover that they have been selling magazines *door-to-door* for nearly 25 years.

Do you see an opportunity here?

In a stroke of genius, you contact the CEO of the company and inform him that you could easily increase their bottom line, single-handedly, by opening their business to a larger market. You then explain in great detail the problems you had when selling door-to-door, and how you finally came up with a solution that would be beneficial not only for you, but for them as well. You see, when *you* make money, *they* make money. So any sane business will gladly jump on an offer that allows them to make more money than before, especially if it doesn't require much more effort on their part.

You begin to explain to the CEO how you are experienced in, say, mail order. You then tell him exactly what steps you would take in order to expand his business to a much larger market through the use of direct selling by mail. In closing, you tell him that you will single-handedly head up his new direct marketing department in return for 40 percent of each subscription sold through those means.

Jackpot! You have just accomplished the following:

➤ Made yourself a well-positioned authority figure in a 25-year-old successful business.

➤ Eliminated the possibility of any competition with your fellow co-workers.

➤ Gotten a *huge* pay raise and the respect and admiration of the CEO.

➤ Become a radical super-affiliate of that company (the *only* one).

And you accomplished all of this because you did a little research, and spotted an opportunity in the making.

Now let's take this analogy a little further. Let's say that you don't know anything about mail order and, although you want to take advantage of this opportunity, you don't have a clue how to operate a successful mail order business. So what can you do? Simple: You take advantage of the hundreds of books written by highly successful mail order marketers, and you *learn*. Information is available on just about anything pertaining to making money. All you have to do is find it, read it, and learn it.

So you can't contact the company's CEO to tell him about your amazing new opportunity for him to make more money while giving you a huge boost in respect, authority, and profits—yet. Keep working for the company, doing the best you can, while you buy the books on mail order marketing and learn what it takes to become successful at it.

But you must envision your end goal: "I want to make more money than ever before." Keep this in mind while working the 9-to-5 door-to-door job. It'll help keep you focused on studying about how to become a successful mail order marketer so that when the time comes, you can finally break free and give the CEO the good news about a new direct marketing department.

Now let's fast-forward six months into the future. You've read the books, studied the material, and maybe even tested it out on some small projects with a little success. Now you know exactly how to run a successful mail order business, and *now* you can approach Mr. CEO to tell him about your offer! All it took was a radically different idea, a little effort, and a little time and you are now known as the person responsible for single-handedly increasing Jason's Business Monthly from 12,000 subscribers to over 130,000 subscribers, all earning you a huge commission check each month from your new direct marketing department of a successful 25-year-old company!

I can hear your doubts: "That's all great and wonderful, but I don't have a door-to-door job and I don't care to know anything about mail order marketing. Can you still help me?"

Yes, I can. I used the above analogy only as an example to get you in the right mind-set for what I am about to explain. Now I will show you how you can take this analogy and adapt it to the Internet to generate huge commission checks online, with virtually any business you want!

■ A SIMPLE FORMULA FOR CREATING RADICAL SUPER-AFFILIATE SUCCESS

In this section you will learn how to spot an opportunity in the making from almost any online business, and take advantage of it in the best possible way. But first, let me tell you a little bit about myself. I am a 22-year-old entrepreneur who has quickly become a well-respected member of the Internet marketing elite. Using the same formula that I will describe here, I have secured my position as vice president and affiliate marketing director of Jo Han Mok's Super Fast Profit enterprise (www.superfastprofit.com) and director of hypnotic design for Joe Vitale's Hypnotic Marketing Institute (www.hypnoticmarketinginstitute.com). Jo Han and Joe have since become great friends of mine, as well as my full-time business partners.

So I'm just a 22-year-old guy who used the knowledge he learned from the marketing masters to spot a huge opportunity in the making, and took immediate advantage of it. This is a big blessing for me, but anyone can do it. Just follow this extremely simplified formula:

Think radically different + a little effort + a little time
= Radical super-affiliate success

Now let's talk about what it takes to become a radical super-affiliate. We'll start with an online version of the previous analogy. Let's say you've had very little experience with copywriting, or maybe none at all. You are currently an affiliate of Jason's Marketing Center, a password-protected site that charges a one-time fee of $39.95 for private access. Jason, the CEO, has been in business for about six months and is trying everything he can to make this a lucrative business venture for himself. He has added valuable content to his private site, and even has a free e-book library that contains hundreds of e-books and marketing manuals designed to help people make money online.

Did you spot the killer opportunity in this story? How could you possibly help this guy?

Easy—here's how: You do your research and find out about Jason's will to succeed, simply by becoming a member of his private site yourself. Then you study his content, his presentation, and his sales letter. You discover that his sales copy is a little weak in some areas and could use some polishing. So you pull out the e-books on copywriting that you've bought in the past, shake off the digital dust, and get to work. Before you contact him, you rewrite his sales letter completely.

Then you decide to get even more creative and think of some extra ideas that could make Jason's business even more profitable. Here is a perfect example: You could rewrite the sales letter from scratch, and instead of making it a one-time fee of $39.95 for a private site, you could make it a private membership with a charge of $19.95 per month. In order to do this, you must make sure Jason's content is always fresh and up-to-date every month. So you will want to find some new way of doing that *for him.* If you don't have a clue how to run a successful membership site, find an e-book on it, read it, learn it, and apply it. The key is to think of Jason's business as if it were your own.

Once you are finished with the sales letter, make sure it has no typos or formatting errors of any kind. Run it through a good spell-checker before you send it off. You could also examine Jason's graphic design for the site, and if it looks like it could use a little work, then either redo it yourself (if you're good at that sort of thing) or just purchase a professional-looking template for the site. Remember, this is now your baby too.

I understand that this may be a lot of work to do before you ever contact anyone, but trust me—if your work is at all better than what Jason has on his site, he will gladly jump on your offer.

You finally finish the new sales letter, your proposal for a new twist on his old idea, and you are ready to make your offer. So you shoot him an e-mail saying something like this:

Subject: Jason, I need to talk with you ASAP.

Hi Jason,

This is John Smith. I have been an affiliate of Jason's Marketing Center for about two months now, and finally decided to take the plunge and see what your private site was all about. Now, I wish that I would've been a member on the first day of becoming an affiliate! Great stuff!

The reason I am writing you is that I have been looking over the content you have provided, and I've noticed that some of it is a little outdated. This is not a problem though, because I would like the chance to fix this for you, permanently. I have devised a unique method of keeping your content fresh and updated constantly, and at the same time making you more money from your site than ever before. And it's not going to cost you a dime.

I have also gone to the trouble of writing another sales letter for you, conveying the new ideas for the site. After you read it, I think you will agree that this would be an excellent opportunity for us both to make a lot more money from this venture than we are making now—you as the owner, and me as the radical super-affiliate.

I have attached a ZIP file of the sales letter in HTML for your viewing pleasure. If you like it, and appreciate all the hard work that went into creating it for you, then please either write me back at john@smith.com or call me at 555-555-5555 to discuss further arrangements.

I do realize that you are a busy person, and so before you read the new sales letter, I just want you to know that any new ideas that are presented in it, I will gladly take care of myself. So you will not have to do one bit of extra work and will still be able to make more money than ever before with your site. Just please read the sales letter to find out what I'm talking about.

Thank you very much for your time.

To your success,

John Smith

E-mail: john@smith.com

Phone: 555-555-5555

P.S. To make it even easier for you, if you would rather I call you, just write back with your phone number and the best time for us to talk.

Now, I want you to carefully study this letter and see if you can point out every hidden suggestion in it. Hidden suggestions are subtle hints in your copy that have the ability to influence the reader to do something.

Hypnotic copywriting is beyond the scope of this chapter, but I just wanted to give you an idea of how you could structure your letter to achieve the desired response—in this case, to get Jason to read your new sales letter and get him to respond to your offer by either replying to your e-mail or calling you personally.

Notice how the letter in no way resembles spam. It looks more like a letter written from one guy to another and contains gratitude (cater to the person's ego), good business sense, and maybe even a little humor. Not too much, just enough to make your letter sound like it came from a friend and not from a businessperson without a soul. There isn't even a disclaimer anywhere that says something like "This letter is not spam." If you've ever gotten an e-mail with those words, you know what I'm talking about—and yes, nine times out of ten it is spam.

Try your best not to make the subject sound anything remotely like spam. With today's growing e-technology, it can be difficult at times to tell whether an e-mail is spam or not. Most autoresponders these days are able to customize an e-mail with the reader's first name in the subject as well as the body of the letter. I look out for something like "Jason, get your *free* . . ." or some other blatant attempt to get me to open the spammer's letter. Some even start off their subject line with "Jason, this is *not* spam."

Do not make an offer of any kind in the subject line of your e-mail. Instead, try a different approach. Something like "Joshua, I have a question" almost always works, because honest business owners like to help out their prospects and customers as much as possible, as it could mean more sales for them.

The letter is very powerful not only because of the way it was presented and structured, but also because you showed Jason that you are serious about helping him make more money from his site with the sales letter you prewrote and then attached for him to see. This establishes immediate credibility in the eyes and mind of Jason, and if your new ideas fly with him and he likes the sales letter you created for him, then you're in business!

You now have the upper hand. You have just proven to Jason that you know your stuff and have thereby positioned yourself as a point of authority in his mind. In another words, he'll begin to look to you from now on for advice about how to make his business more profitable.

After you send your message, expect either an e-mail or a direct phone call from him to talk about your offer. When this happens, keep a professional yet friendly attitude *at all times*. The last thing you want to do is to make a fool of yourself by overreacting. Keep it as professional as possible, and he will become even more entranced by the perceived image you are creating in his mind. Don't lie to him or pretend to be something you're not. Just be yourself. Be human, as he is human. Master the idea behind the following statement, and you can conquer the world:

No matter how rich or famous people are, they are still human and are bound by the same basic needs and wants as you have. You are only limited to the extent that you limit yourself. So remove your limits and create your reality.

—Jason Mangrum

Back to the story . . . Finally, the e-mail arrives:

Subject: Re: Jason, I need to talk with you ASAP.

You carefully scan each and every word of his reply, and to your utter amazement, he wholeheartedly thanks you for your time and effort, and accepts your offer! He says that he is very grateful for your taking the time to help him, and he would like to know what you would want in return for such a great favor. This is where your palms can get a little sweaty. What do you write back?

Take some time to relax, breathe deeply, and calm your racing mind.

When you formulate your reply, take into account the amount of work you will have to do and how much time you will have to spend on keeping Jason's site freshly updated. Also take into account how much Jason will now be charging for his new site. In your reply, state the facts about the amount of time and effort you will be putting into his new business. Then reassure him that he will be making more money per customer even though he lowered his price, because the customer will automatically be billed $19.95 per month, instead of only $39.95 for one sale.

Then state your desired percentage—let's say 40 percent of all profits made through the new and improved site. This is where things can get tricky, because the minute you mention money, people will start analyzing everything you say—especially if you're talking about *taking* someone's money. So be very careful with this part.

To immediately counteract any concerns that Jason might have, you can provide a few facts. All you'll need is a little creativity and a calculator. Let's say Jason has a total of 153 members at his private site (the old one).

$$153 \times \$39.95 = \$6,112.35 \text{ one-time profit} = \$0 \text{ per month} = \$0 \text{ per year}$$

With the new plan, if he could just get another 153 members to join his new private site, the figures would dramatically change:

$$153 \times \$19.95 = \$3,052.35 \text{ per month} = \$36,628.20 \text{ per year}$$

In return for your services, you're asking only 40 percent of the overall profits, so your cut would be $1,220.80 per month or $14,649.60 per year.

I can still hear you thinking, "But that's not the kind of money I want to make. I can't get rich making only $14,649 a year. I can barely live on that."

Yes, that's true. However, you're forgetting one very important point here: The point is that this is only one business out of the thousands of online businesses that could use your help and your radical thinking. You won't have to spend more than two days a month to find the material and keep Jason's site updated every month. Just two days out of the entire month is now making you a cool $14,649 a year in extra cash that you wouldn't have had before.

One down, the rest of the Internet to go. As you begin to notice the powerful implications of this profit-pulling strategy, you may also begin to realize that you can do this with *any* business, large or small. I have used a story to keep you interested in my message and to take you through each step in a way you will remember easily. But the truth is, this can be done with any business, even if it is not Internet marketing related at all.

Say you have come across a web site that sells an e-book of recipes. The product sells for $17 and is doing pretty well. However, one basic desire that we all have in common is the desire to make more money. So you do some research on becoming a consultant, and then approach the author of the book with an offer to create a private cooking consultation service for $20 a month. Or you could create a private e-class on "Specialty Cooking" for $100 per person—of course, using *her* material and *your* radically different thinking.

You may be thinking "$100 per person for a *cooking class*? You're out of your mind. No one would ever pay $100 for a cooking class!" That may or may not be true. To an extremely targeted market, full of professional cooks and wannabes, a six-week e-class featuring personal, one-on-one consultation may not be a bad deal for $100. That's not my point. If you want to learn all about e-classes, buy Joe Vitale's book on them.

However, my point is that all the greatest people in the world had one thing in common: They thought radically differently from anyone else. In doing so, they positioned themselves and their name high among all the billions of other people in history.

As I begin to come to a close, I will leave you with one final thought. You have actually seen me use this hidden technique throughout this chapter. You just haven't noticed it, because it's a *hidden* technique. Of course, the technique I am speaking of is called *positioning.*

Positioning is a very subtle yet extremely powerful approach to gaining the upper hand in almost every situation. It doesn't matter if you are actually better, faster, stronger, or more intelligent than your competitors. All that matters is that you make them think you are. Now, I'm in no way saying you need to lie to them. I'm not implying that at all. What I'm saying is that you are what you are *perceived* to be in the minds of others.

So put in some effort, work smart—not hard—and think radically differently from anyone else, and you will automatically be looked up to as an authority figure on any particular subject you choose. This is exactly how it was done in the stories I have told you in this chapter, and exactly how you can do it too, with any business you want. Just look for the opportunity in the making. If necessary, learn about it and apply it, and then go out and make it happen. Then replicate it again and again, until you are completely satisfied with your radical super-affiliate income and status. Remember:

A big idea + a little effort + a little time
= Radical super-affiliate success

As this chapter finally comes to a close, I'll give you a perfect illustration of positioning. I knew there were going to be many other top marketers in this book. I knew that if I didn't think radically differently about how to present my message, I would just be known as another marketer writing a chapter in a book. So, as you can see, I did something radically different. And all it took was three extra words and a small request.

I simply requested that the creators of the book place my chapter at the very end of the book. Then I added only three extra words to my headline to make it read "Special Bonus Chapter: Confessions of a Radical Super-Affiliate." This way, everyone reading this book (including you) will pay special attention to my chapter, simply because it includes the words "Special Bonus Chapter." This gives the book added value, and at the same time positions me as a point of authority in the mind of the reader.

I have even used a hidden positioning technique to brand my name throughout this chapter. Notice how many times I used the name Jason as I wrote. I did this purposely so that you will remember me more easily. Also, since I have written the last chapter of this book, my message will be fresh in your mind—but so will be the name Jason Mangrum.

Jason Mangrum is a young genius at web design and web marketing. He does sites for web gurus, such as Joe Vitale. He's at www.immwebdesign.com.

About the Authors

Dr. Joe Vitale is the world's first hypnotic marketer and an Internet marketing pioneer. He is the president of Hypnotic Marketing Inc. and the author of too many books to list here, including *The Attractor Factor*, the best-selling *Spiritual Marketing*, the best-selling e-book *Hypnotic Writing*, and the best-selling Nightingale-Conant audio program, "The Power of Outrageous Marketing." His latest book is the best-selling *The Greatest Money Making Secret in History*. Sign up for his free newsletter at www.MrFire.com.

Jo Han Mok is a popular featured speaker at Internet marketing bootcamps as the "Singapore Star of Joint Ventures and Free Advertising." He has shared the stage with luminaries like Ted Ciuba, Joe Vitale, Armand Morin, Peter Sun, Randy Charach, Carl Galleti, Kirt Christensen, Alex Mandossian, Frank Garon, Jeff Gardner, Michael Penland, David Garfinkel, Mike Stewart, Bill Harris, Brad Antin, Mal Emery, Brett McFall, Tom Hua, Paul Barrs, David Cavanagh, and too many others to list here. He is also a highly sought after Internet marketing consultant and is widely regarded as one of the top copywriters in the world. Find out how his unique system takes scraggly rookies by the hand and turns them into world-class Internet marketers. Go to http://www.PowerAffiliateMarketing.com.

Index

271